The 5-Minute BIBLE STUDY for Men

Mornings in God's Word

D1637412

Print ISBN 978-1-63609-203-4

Cover Photograph: Dominik Reallife, Unsplash

Published by Barbour Publishing, Inc., 1810 Barbour Drive, Uhrichsville, Ohio 44683, www.barbourbooks.com

Our mission is to inspire the world with the life-changing message of the Bible.

Member of the
Evangelical Christian
Publishers Association

Ed Cyzewski

The 5-Minute BIBLE STUDY for Men

Mornings in God's Word

BARBOUR PUBLISHING

Introduction

The pages of scripture offer assurance that God will remain near to the faithful even when life isn't smooth sailing. If your heart is devoted to the Lord, you have the assurance of comfort and support through the storms of life. Getting a jump start to your day in the pages of scripture can prove to be one of the most effective ways to ensure that you remain aware of God and faithful to your call as God's beloved child no matter what your day brings.

Scripture can be a map that ensures you remain on course, never straying far from the place where you can sense the Holy Spirit's still small voice. As your heart drifts after one thing or your mind obsesses about another, the steady guidance of scripture can help you remain oriented in the way that keeps the Lord in view.

Men can face a barrage of expectations and demands from different segments of society that can feel overwhelming and even conflicting at times. They are expected to provide and protect while also nurturing and providing comfort. Temptations abound, and the lure of a carefree, self-centered life surely beckons. Yet in the stillness and silence of the present moment, the whisper of God the Father is calling His sons to be still and at rest.

The invitation of God's presence and abundance is for you. Jesus promised His living water of life to all who thirst, and if your desire is for God, then all you need to bring is an attentive mind and an open heart. God's unimaginable love is yours if you will become present for it, and this devotional offers one of many ways to do so.

This devotional guide is a starting point for becoming still before your loving Father, selecting a wide variety of scriptures that are ideal for personal study and meditation. You'll cover the entire sweep of biblical history and walk alongside God's people, gaining insight and wisdom for your own life. Each selection comes from a larger portion of scripture that you can read in your own Bible, and then a series of questions in the "Understand" section will help you ponder the meaning and message of that passage.

A brief reflection then offers a few points of application to your life today, revealing the Bible's relevance and power for the present moment. Each devotion ends with a prayer that will help you bring your own concerns and challenges before God. While each devotion aims to take only five minutes of your time, my hope is that you'll use this series of devotions as a starting point for longer moments of quiet devotion, reflection, and prayer.

God's Direction Makes Courageous Decisions Possible

—————— READ JOSHUA 1:1–7 ——————

KEY VERSES

"Be strong and courageous, for you shall give this people possession of the land which I swore to their fathers to give them. Only be strong and very courageous; be careful to do according to all the Law which Moses My servant commanded you; do not turn from it to the right or to the left, so that you may achieve success wherever you go."

JOSHUA 1:6–7 NASB

UNDERSTAND

+ How does God's promise to Israel relate to the command to be strong and courageous?

+ Why is obedience to the Law paired with the command to be courageous?

+ How does God measure success in this exchange with Joshua? How does that compare to the ways that success is measured today?

APPLY

In Exodus 33:11, we read that Joshua didn't depart from the tabernacle even after Moses retired for the evening. As Joshua was set to take charge of God's people, those quiet moments with the Lord started to pay off as he received His charge to "be strong and very courageous" during a time of uncertainty and conflict.

Taking quiet moments to be present with the Lord lays a foundation of attention to His voice and obedience to His commands that will be essential in your life today. The Lord's command to Joshua wasn't a general admonishment to be strong and courageous. He received a specific charge from God, and because he heard God's commands, he could confidently make the difficult and dangerous decisions ahead.

Your own challenge today is to discern what God is asking of you and to be receptive to the teachings of scripture. When you have confidence in God's calling and direction for you, it will be far easier to make the tough decisions that require courage and strength.

PRAY

Father, I ask that You would meet me in the private, quiet moments of my life and that I would hear Your voice calling me to pause and listen even during the storms of life. Help me to respond to today's challenges with faith and courage. Amen.

Love Is Real Freedom

—— READ GALATIANS 5:13–18 ——

KEY VERSES

*For you have been called to live in freedom,
my brothers and sisters. But don't use your
freedom to satisfy your sinful nature. Instead,
use your freedom to serve one another in love.
For the whole law can be summed up in this one
command: "Love your neighbor as yourself."*
GALATIANS 5:13–14 NLT

UNDERSTAND

+ What does freedom mean to you right now?
  How does Paul want Christians to understand
  freedom and use it as a guide in their lives?

+ Consider how you can depend on the Holy
  Spirit today to guide you through the competing
  desires to use your freedom either for your own
  indulgence or for loving service of others.

+ How can a healthy love of yourself guide you
  today in making choices that benefit others?

APPLY

In today's passage, Paul was asking who guides
your life and whether you are using your freedom
and gifts for your own sake or for the sake of your
neighbors. If you allow the Holy Spirit to guide you,
there's a good chance you'll be able to make choices

that benefit yourself, benefit others, and lead you toward real freedom in Christ.

The problem is that "freedom" is often portrayed as doing what you want when you want regardless of how it impacts your neighbors. Even worse, this self-indulgence is a short-term path to peace and contentment, so self-centered freedom can become a trap that holds you back from God and others.

You have an open invitation today to ask God's Spirit to guide you, to entrust yourself to the safest, surest guide to freedom and joy. Today you can discover that God's Spirit leads you to freedom you could have never found on your own.

PRAY

Holy Spirit, thank You for Your presence in my life and for Your compassion for me. Help me to see the ways I can remain aware of others and use my freedom to love and serve them. May I see the dead ends of personal indulgence today so that I can remain free in You. Amen.

God Knows Your Needs
before You Pray

———— READ MATTHEW 6:1–8 ————

KEY VERSES

*"But when you pray, go into your room, close
the door and pray to your Father, who is unseen.
Then your Father, who sees what is done in
secret, will reward you. And when you pray, do
not keep on babbling like pagans, for they think
they will be heard because of their many words."*
MATTHEW 6:6–7 NIV

UNDERSTAND

+ What do you long to receive as a result of your
  prayers and your Christian practices? How can
  you guard against craving accolades from others
  and instead trust God to be present and concerned about you when you pray?

+ Why do you think it's so important to Jesus that
  you pray and practice your good deeds in secret?

+ What are your expectations when you begin to
  pray? How could starting out with confidence
  that God knows exactly what you need change
  the way you pray?

APPLY

How often do you see results right away when you
pray? Prayer isn't a practice that usually brings immediate rewards or benefits. Instead, it's a long-term

investment in a relationship with God. Oftentimes a prayer may be answered in an unexpected way or on a timeline that is quite different from your own. It's tempting to see prayer and other spiritual practices as signs of your own holiness and goodness before others.

Today Jesus asks you to take a big leap of faith, to trust that God not only hears your prayers and sees your good deeds but also knows exactly what you need before you even ask. When you do that, God will reward you for what you do in private, seen by Him alone. That calls for a lot of waiting and a lot of trust.

Even though God knows what you need, Jesus wants you to release your concerns and requests to Him. When you pray, you cultivate a relationship with God, one that benefits you as you share your hopes, fears, and concerns with Him. Not only that, but you make yourself available to God in the secret, quiet place. The benefits of doing these things are beyond what you can imagine.

PRAY

Father, I trust that You know what I need before I ask and that You will reward me for what I do for You and for others in secret. May I turn my gaze away from what I can gain from others right now and instead entrust myself to Your kindness and generosity as I pray. Amen.

Hope in God Brings Gladness

———— READ PSALM 33:13–22 ————

KEY VERSES

Our soul waits for the LORD; he is our help and
shield. Our heart is glad in him, because we
trust in his holy name. Let your steadfast love,
O LORD, be upon us, even as we hope in you.
PSALM 33:20–22 NRSV

UNDERSTAND

+ How would you describe your heart or emotions
  right now? What would you like to ask God to
  change?

+ In whom or what do you most often find yourself
  placing your trust? How can you increase your
  hope and trust in God?

+ Consider whether you're aware of God's love for
  you today. How does today's passage encourage
  you to think of God's love for you?

APPLY

Today's reading is about adversity and about whom
you depend on in the midst of it. Consider how
people—those in your immediate circles and those in
the wider culture—handle adversity and challenges.
Who or what are they relying on for their hope?

Rather than looking at the size of the challenges
before you today, consider that God is looking down
on you and on everyone else from heaven. God has

fashioned the hearts of men and knows everyone's secret deeds. When you rely on God and fear Him, you can count on Him seeing and caring for you in the midst of your adversity.

What you focus on today will go a long way toward determining your relationship with God. Today's reading ends with an image of God's love resting on His people. That can be a source of comfort for you today as you face challenges and adversity. If you depend on God and look to Him as your source of hope, you will find security and peace in the most challenging of times.

PRAY

Father, You are greater than anyone or anything, and Your power is unmatched. May I find peace, hope, and gladness in Your presence and power today, waiting patiently for Your intervention in my life. May Your steadfast love rest on me and my loved ones. Amen.

Pray for Those Who Are Suffering

———— READ NEHEMIAH 1 ————

KEY VERSES

"Remember, please, the word which You commanded Your servant Moses, saying, 'If you are unfaithful, I will scatter you among the peoples; but if you return to Me and keep My commandments and do them, though those of you who have been scattered were in the most remote part of the heavens, I will gather them from there and bring them to the place where I have chosen to have My name dwell.'"
NEHEMIAH 1:8–9 NASB

UNDERSTAND

* What can you learn about the people of Israel in this passage? How did Nehemiah act toward them in response to their situation?

* What does this passage teach about obedience versus disobedience and the consequences God's people faced for their actions?

* It appeared that the worst had happened to the people of Israel. How did Nehemiah go about making things right with God?

APPLY

Consider those who are suffering or struggling today. They may be facing the consequences of their actions, or they may be swept up into circumstances beyond their control. Suffering and loss happen for a variety of reasons. Regardless, Nehemiah saw that the people of Israel were suffering because of their unfaithfulness but still interceded in prayer for them.

Nehemiah was the cupbearer to King Artaxerxes of Persia, and he had every reason to focus on the seemingly more important issues of the palace. Although he lived in a foreign land, he had comfort and influence. Yet he took time to learn about the remnant living in Israel, and he prayed with compassion for them when he learned of their suffering. His example is a reminder to show concern for those suffering regardless of their circumstances, especially if you are living in comfort and plenty.

Nehemiah's intercession for his people is also worthy of notice because he modeled an awareness of God's commands, a humility in acknowledging the sin of Israel, and a plea for mercy based on God's character. As you intercede for yourself and for others, Nehemiah's prayer is a good example of repentance and of full trust in God.

PRAY

*Father, You will not abandon Your people
to their sins and failures if they repent and
pray. I ask for Your mercy for my faults.
May I show awareness and compassion
toward others who are suffering shame
and deprivation today. Amen.*

Humility Is Tied to God's Provision

—— READ DEUTERONOMY 8:1–10 ——

KEY VERSE

*"Yes, he humbled you by letting you go hungry and then feeding you with manna, a food previously unknown to you and your ancestors. He did it to teach you that people do not live by bread alone; rather, we live by every word that comes from the mouth of the L*ORD*."*

DEUTERONOMY 8:3 NLT

UNDERSTAND

+ Why is humility so important for those who want to receive God's provision?

+ While everyone needs a source of income in order to eat, what does it mean to you that people don't live by "bread alone"?

+ What would it look like today for you to more completely depend on every word from the mouth of God?

APPLY

No one enjoys being humbled or disciplined, but today's scripture reading shares how God taught the people of Israel to depend more completely on Him. The process wasn't easy or pleasant—in fact, it involved a lot of fear and uncertainty in a hostile wilderness. God's method of provision was a complete unknown, a new kind of bread they had never tasted delivered in a most unusual way.

Yet on the other side of that difficult, humbling experience, the people of Israel started to learn to depend on God and to examine their hearts so that they turned only to Him and to no one else.

You may be in the midst of some uncertainty or an unfamiliar situation in which you don't know how things are going to turn out. This gives you an opportunity to humble yourself before God and to grow in your dependence and obedience.

The outcome of humbling experiences, or of God's discipline, may not be what you prefer in the moment, but you can be assured that depending on Him for your daily provision and care will lead to praise and gratitude. There is hope for you on the other side of life's lowest moments—if you can learn to seek God alone when all else remains uncertain.

PRAY

Father, You have promised both to humble me and to be present for me in life's challenges. May I learn to depend on You for my daily provision and care rather than relying on what I can control and what I can do on my own. I trust that You can provide for my needs in the most unlikely and unexpected ways. Amen.

What Are You Asking God For?

————— READ JAMES 4:1–10 —————

KEY VERSES

You desire but do not have, so you kill. You covet but you cannot get what you want, so you quarrel and fight. You do not have because you do not ask God. When you ask, you do not receive, because you ask with wrong motives, that you may spend what you get on your pleasures.

JAMES 4:2–3 NIV

UNDERSTAND

+ What types of desires was James addressing in this passage? How can desires become positive—and how can they become destructive?

+ James was concerned both with *what* you ask God to do and *how* you ask Him to do it. What does the right kind of asking look like in your life?

+ James wrote of the importance of humility and submission to God. What do you need to submit to God today?

APPLY

James invites you to examine your desires and the way you approach getting what you want. Your desires can be the catalyst for conflict that alienates you from others and prevents you from enjoying true intimacy with God.

Those who resist God leave themselves vulnerable to other influences that can send their lives into conflict. Humble submission means that you are no longer holding on to what you demand, and that frees you to receive from God. As you draw near to God, you'll have fewer conflicts with others.

Submission to God isn't easy. James described it as a battle for good reason. It may be a lifelong process rather than a quick fix you enact today. Yet, as you pray today, tomorrow, and the rest of this week, you can ask God whether you have laid down your desires to Him—and whether your motives in prayer are in line with God's best for you.

As you go about your day, examine what you desire and whether you have placed your desires in God's care.

PRAY

Father, examine my heart and reveal my inner motives and desires with Your light so that I can seek what is best for You, for myself, and for others. May I see the ways my heart can become divided, and may I become a person of peace who can release his own desires to You. Amen.

The Source of Peace with God

———— READ ROMANS 5:1–11 ————

KEY VERSES

*For if while we were enemies we were reconciled
to God through the death of His Son, much more,
having been reconciled, we shall be saved by
His life. And not only this, but we also celebrate
in God through our Lord Jesus Christ, through
whom we have now received the reconciliation.*
ROMANS 5:10–11 NASB

UNDERSTAND

- Do you feel "worthy" of God today? What does today's scripture passage say about your standing before God?
- Think about a time when you've been reconciled with someone after a failure or dispute. According to this passage, what does reconciliation with God look like?
- Paul described being transformed from being an enemy against God to celebrating reconciliation with Him. Which do you relate to more right now? How can this passage help you shift your understanding?

APPLY

Today you can fully enjoy and celebrate reconciliation with God. Many generations ago, Paul wrote today's passage and made it clear that God wants to be reconciled with you.

God's love is with you because He sent His Son, Jesus, to earth to bring about reconciliation between Himself and humanity. You can't undermine God's mercy, because Jesus arrived while you and every other human who had lived or would ever live here on earth were still sinners. If you understand that you are a sinner right now, the good news is that you qualify for God's reconciling work.

Your only action right now is to have faith in Jesus, trusting God to change you in ways you could never change yourself. This was a calling you were never able to fulfill on your own. Yet God's love and mercy have lifted you out of conflict with Him and restored you to a place of peace and blessing.

PRAY

Jesus, thank You for Your love, mercy, and kindness, which You put on display in Your life, death, and resurrection here on earth. I am grateful to be healed, restored, and forgiven for my sins, grateful that I can trust in You without fear or reservation. May I fully live in the love You have poured out in my heart through Your Holy Spirit. Amen.

Remembering God's Promises

—— READ 1 KINGS 8:25–32 ——

KEY VERSES

"May you watch over this Temple night and day, this place where you have said, 'My name will be there.' May you always hear the prayers I make toward this place. May you hear the humble and earnest requests from me and your people Israel when we pray toward this place. Yes, hear us from heaven where you live, and when you hear, forgive."

1 KINGS 8:29–30 NLT

UNDERSTAND

- Consider the promises Solomon brought to people's minds when he began the prayer to God recorded in today's scripture reading. What is the value of including a "reminder" of God's past promises while praying?
- Solomon asked God to watch over the temple day and night. Why would he make a point of asking Him to do that even if Israel could claim to be God's people?
- What did Solomon's prayer anticipate about God's people in the future? In light of that, how should God's people respond?

APPLY

As you begin your day, Solomon's approach to prayer in today's scripture reading offers some practical guidance for your prayers: claiming God's promises for you, trusting in God's faithfulness and watchfulness, and then relying on God's mercy to restore you after failure. You may have moments of failure or struggle today, but you can follow Solomon's example by humbly praying for restoration.

Wrapped up in this prayer is the possibility of doubt. You may enter this day with lingering doubts about God's care for you, or you may worry that God will disown you if you fall into sin. It should offer you a comfort that Solomon fully expected the people of Israel to fail and to need God's restoration. By relying on God's promises, he models a way to pray with faith and boldness.

Don't miss the fact that this was a public prayer in front of the whole nation—a prayer that was recorded for future generations. It may not be comfortable to admit that you or your own people will have failures to confess in the future, but this corporate humility was surely appropriate and is worth imitating.

PRAY

Father, You know that I may fail and struggle today, but I will trust in Your mercy and kindness and rely on the promises You have given me in Jesus. May I remain humble as I seek Your forgiveness and restoration. Amen.

Healed through Intercession

— READ 2 CHRONICLES 30:13–20 —

KEY VERSES

Hezekiah prayed for them, saying, "May the LORD, who is good, pardon everyone who sets their heart on seeking God—the LORD, the God of their ancestors—even if they are not clean according to the rules of the sanctuary." And the LORD heard Hezekiah and healed the people.
2 CHRONICLES 30:18–20 NIV

UNDERSTAND

- The people of Israel were starting over with God after making many mistakes along the way. How have guilt and shame over your past sins kept you away from God, and what can you do about it?
- Today's scripture passage records Hezekiah's intercessory prayer for people who were sincerely seeking God but still breaking the rules. What does this show you about imperfect men seeking a perfect God?
- Why is intercession so important for God's people?

APPLY

You are never too far from God that you can't start over by repenting and seeking to make things right. If you're dealing with guilt, shame, or the consequences of your past failures—even if they happened in the past twenty-four hours—God gives you the opportunity to begin anew with Him. The Lord longs to pardon the sins of His people when they humble themselves before Him.

The key here is that you need to make changes when you repent. The people of Israel did that when they got rid of the idols and other objects that had tripped them up. The status quo won't cut it, but if you're willing to reach out to God in sincere devotion, He welcomes even your imperfect prayers.

King Hezekiah modeled a pure spirit of intercession when he asked God to show mercy on his people rather than smugly dismissing those who failed to observe purity laws. In doing that, he showed that God will honor the prayers of His people on behalf of others and that His mercy will triumph when we pray.

PRAY

Father, reveal the shame and failures in my life that have kept me from You so that I can worship You without fear, discouragement, or self-condemnation. May I be a voice of encouragement and grace to those in need of healing and restoration, showing mercy even as You have shown mercy to me. Amen.

The Ultimate Choice in Life

———— READ LUKE 9:21–27 ————

KEY VERSES

> *"If you try to hang on to your life, you*
> *will lose it. But if you give up your life*
> *for my sake, you will save it. And what do*
> *you benefit if you gain the whole world*
> *but are yourself lost or destroyed?"*
>
> LUKE 9:24–25 NLT

UNDERSTAND

- ♦ Why did Jesus challenge His followers to give up their own lives right after telling them about His own imminent crucifixion and resurrection?
- ♦ What do you think it means to "gain the whole world"?
- ♦ What does it look like to "give up your life" for the sake of Jesus?

APPLY

As Jesus prepared Himself and His disciples for His upcoming death on a wooden cross, He taught them that they too needed to stop hanging on to their own lives. They had a choice to make—between devoting themselves to an uncertain world that leaves their souls in peril or devoting themselves to God and placing their souls in His care.

This is an invitation to look at the direction of your life. Each little choice you make every day will contribute to where you end up in life's journey.

Where can you let go of your own desires and priorities and entrust them to God? This calls for ongoing examination and awareness of what goes into your choices each day.

Most importantly, remember that surrendering your life to the Lord comes with a no-doubt-about-it reward. While there are no guarantees regarding your own safety and security here on earth, your soul is safe with God, and no one can touch the reward He has promised you.

PRAY

> *Jesus, help me to see the areas of my life where I've sought control or failed to entrust myself to You. May I enjoy the rewards of faith and obedience as I choose life in You over anything else this world may offer. Amen.*

God Uses the Evil Done to Us for Good

———— READ GENESIS 50:15–21 ————

KEY VERSES

But Joseph said to them, "Do not be afraid, for am I in God's place? As for you, you meant evil against me, but God meant it for good in order to bring about this present result, to keep many people alive."
GENESIS 50:19–20 NASB

UNDERSTAND

- Joseph's brothers had dealt treacherously with him in the past, and even here they lied about his father's dying wishes in order to spare their own lives. What does this story show about the long-term impact of sin?
- How did Joseph view the evil brought against him?
- Why was the bigger picture of God's work so important for Joseph?

APPLY

It may be difficult to look at the injustices or challenges of your life the way Joseph did. But God has invited you today to entrust yourself to Him and to seek ways He can use even your greatest losses for the benefit of others.

Seeking God at work in a bigger picture, one

you may not fully understand until much later, helps you put less emphasis on the losses, suffering, and mistreatment of today. You will be less likely to hold grudges, because God so often uses even your worst losses for your benefit—and for the benefit of others. There surely will be pain and uncertainty along the way, but when you trust that God is with you, today's circumstances can shift in their significance.

Showing mercy to others is also easier when you recognize that you, like Joseph, aren't God. You have received mercy from the Lord, and it is up to Him alone to judge others. That means you are free from the burden of judgment on others, and you can share the grace and forgiveness you have received.

PRAY

Father, may I always remember the grace and mercy You have shown to me so that I will never hold grudges against others or set myself as a judge over them. May I see Your power at work in my life and respond with faith and hope when challenges surface. Amen.

Free to Bless Others

—— READ ROMANS 12:14–21 ——

KEY VERSES

> *Bless those who persecute you. Don't*
> *curse them; pray that God will bless*
> *them. Be happy with those who are*
> *happy, and weep with those who weep.*
> ROMANS 12:14–15 NLT

UNDERSTAND

* How is treating your enemies or opponents with compassion and understanding an act of faith in God?
* How would it benefit you to bless those who mistreat you?
* In what ways could your day change if you were more aware of the happiness and sadness of others?

APPLY

You could begin today feeling defensive and even combative toward those you perceive as enemies or opponents, or you could begin today by praying for them and resolving to treat them well. How you view and act toward those who are most opposed to you may determine the outcome of the rest of your day!

As long as you are withdrawn from others out of fear, anger, or other negative emotions, you'll never reach them with God's redeeming love—instead, you'll be preoccupied with negative thoughts of them. The path Paul laid out in today's scripture verses is a more constructive and hopeful way forward that frees you from fear and anger and opens up new possibilities for healing and improved relationships.

This is a liberating opportunity to look beyond your own concerns and worries. You can share the joy and sorrow of others, celebrating when appropriate and mourning when difficulties abound. It's possible that those with whom you celebrate and mourn today will do the same for you in the future.

PRAY

Jesus, help me to see all people as made in Your image and to treat opponents and enemies with compassion and consideration. I surrender my fears and distrust of others to You so that I can serve them and treat them with the same kindness I would hope to receive for myself. Amen.

God Loved You First

———— READ 1 JOHN 4:16–21 ————

KEY VERSES

There is no fear in love, but perfect love drives
out fear, because fear involves punishment,
and the one who fears is not perfected in
love. We love, because He first loved us.
1 JOHN 4:18–19 NASB

UNDERSTAND

+ How do you reconcile the concept of "the fear of the Lord" with perfect love driving out fear?
+ Why is it so significant that God loved you first? What is the result of that love for you?
+ Why are loving God and loving others so closely connected?

APPLY

How would your outlook for today change if, before you even got out of bed, you remembered that God loves you deeply and passionately, that He loved you before you could possibly love Him in return.

God's love is a transformational kind of love, and it puts you in a place of security from where you can be freed from the fear of judgment and enabled to imagine new ways of relating to others. If God loves you so much, that also means that He loves the people you encounter each day. God's love may not have shaped every person you meet, and many may have rejected it outright, but each person holds tremendous possibility in God.

John saw loving God as a compelling command-ment that requires His beloved people to love their neighbors. As you prepare to face your day, ask God how you can show His love to the people in your sphere of influence.

PRAY

Father, help me to see with clarity the love that You have so generously shown me. May I live free from fear and approach You in prayer with confidence that Your love has come to me before I could do anything for You in return. May I show Your perfect love to those I meet today. Amen.

Remember What You've Seen

—— READ DEUTERONOMY 4:9–14 ——

KEY VERSES

*But take care and watch yourselves closely,
so as neither to forget the things that your
eyes have seen nor to let them slip from your
mind all the days of your life; make them
known to your children and your children's
children—how you once stood before the LORD
your God at Horeb, when the LORD said to
me, "Assemble the people for me, and I will
let them hear my words, so that they may
learn to fear me as long as they live on the
earth, and may teach their children so."*

DEUTERONOMY 4:9–10 NRSV

UNDERSTAND

♦ What do you think Moses specifically meant when he told the Israelites to "take care and watch yourselves closely"?

♦ What was at stake when the Israelites heard the words of God and repeated them to their children and grandchildren?

♦ What does this passage teach about passing along spiritual experiences and lessons to younger generations?

APPLY

What you experience with God and what you learn about Him today isn't just for your own benefit in the present moment. When you have a significant experience or learn an insight that shapes how you live, you have a holy calling to remember that moment and to pass it along to future generations.

God's teachings are meant to be taken seriously and obeyed. Even the moment of receiving those teachings for the first time is a significant step toward passing them along in the future. Each major step forward or epiphany of God's grace in your life can become an opportunity to pass something vital along to others, including future generations.

Whether or not you have children or grand-children, you have a calling that extends far beyond today. Future generations can benefit from your faithfulness and commitment to the Lord and to His Word.

PRAY

Father, help me to notice what is most important and to remember what You have passed along to me both in my spiritual experiences with You and in my knowledge of Your Word. May I invest in the spiritual health of future generations so that they will never forget how You have revealed Yourself. Amen.

Obedience Calls for Courage

—— READ 2 CHRONICLES 15:1-9 ——

KEY VERSE

When Asa heard these words and the prophecy
of Azariah son of Oded the prophet, he took
courage. He removed the detestable idols from
the whole land of Judah and Benjamin and
from the towns he had captured in the hills of
Ephraim. He repaired the altar of the Lord that
was in front of the portico of the Lord's temple.
2 CHRONICLES 15:8 NIV

UNDERSTAND

♦ King Asa faced a lot of adversity in restoring the
people of Israel. While he received a clear prophetic message about continuing his reform work,
why do you think he needed to be courageous?

♦ What is the significance of the Lord's altar being
in disrepair and then fixing it?

♦ After his repair work, Asa gathered the people
together. What was at stake in this kind of
public gathering?

APPLY

God may not have given you a clear message about
what He wants you to do next, but He has given
you plenty of teachings and commands in scripture
to guide you. Removing any false gods or sources
of comfort and control could be a very practical
place to begin. Or you may need to consider the

places where you worship Him and ask yourself if they are in need of repair.

Whatever your next step is in response to God's teachings or direction in your life, you may need to make some hard choices. You may need to run against the accepted wisdom of the day or even in your community. Making big shifts always requires courage and vision as you look ahead to a promising future that others may not be able to imagine.

Others in your community may not recognize you for your faithfulness, and that's where courage will surely come in handy. If you have a clear vision from God, then you are free to take risks and to see how God's blessings unfold.

PRAY

Father, help me to listen to Your voice in my life and to make the hard choices that remove the obstacles from knowing and loving You as You are worthy. May I repair what is broken down in my worship of You, and may I never give in to the pressure of others but instead remain wholly devoted to You. Amen.

No Good Thing Is Held Back

———— READ PSALM 84:5–12 ————

KEY VERSES

*For a day in Your courtyards is better than
a thousand elsewhere. I would rather stand
at the threshold of the house of my God
than live in the tents of wickedness. For
the LORD God is a sun and shield; the LORD
gives grace and glory; He withholds no good
thing from those who walk with integrity.*

PSALM 84:10–11 NASB

UNDERSTAND

- What benefit does the writer of Psalm 84 seek to gain by dwelling at the entrance to God's house?
- What does it mean for God to be a sun and a shield for His people?
- Why is "walking with integrity" so important for those who want God to withhold "no good thing" from them?

APPLY

You're likely immersed in a culture that is always on the lookout for one more good thing—and then one more good thing. . .and then another. Yet God promises to withhold no good thing from you if you walk with integrity. As you look ahead to your day, you have an opportunity to trust God to generously supply everything you need.

It's possible that you may believe you need more

than what God has given to you. But instead of focusing on what you don't have, you can shift your priorities and spend more time in God's presence and among God's people. When you do that, you'll find more peace and contentment than you could living "in the tents of the wicked."

Contentment isn't easy to find today. But where you spend your time today may prove to be one of the most important factors in determining whether you feel content and at peace with God.

PRAY

Father, thank You for the promise to care for the needs of those who walk with integrity and seek You first by dwelling in Your house. May I find what I need in You and forever leave behind the empty promises found among those who seek only their own satisfaction. Amen.

Look toward the Unseen

—— READ 2 CORINTHIANS 4:11–18 ——

KEY VERSES

For our present troubles are small and won't last very long. Yet they produce for us a glory that vastly outweighs them and will last forever! So we don't look at the troubles we can see now; rather, we fix our gaze on things that cannot be seen. For the things we see now will soon be gone, but the things we cannot see will last forever.

2 CORINTHIANS 4:17–18 NLT

UNDERSTAND

- How do you typically evaluate the size of the troubles you are facing right now? What kind of shift did Paul suggest in today's verses?
- What is the challenge of focusing on the things that you can't see right now?
- How can you strike a balance between an awareness of God's rewards for today's faithfulness and being present in the challenges of the moment?

APPLY

You are right to take the troubles you face today seriously, and you should give them your full consideration. The pain and exhaustion of challenges and suffering can take a very real toll. You should also respond with empathy and care to the difficulties others face.

Yet when you step back from the immediacy of the moment and read today's scripture verses, you'll see that Paul offered another viewpoint. You can look at today through God's eternal lens, seeing how each small choice and action impacts your enjoyment of the new life. The more you learn to value the things of God's kingdom today, the more you'll find contentment in Him.

This is a moment for encouragement and hope even in dark, uncertain times. God hasn't forgotten you. Persevering today and remaining present in His will has far-reaching ramifications that you can only imagine on this side of heaven.

PRAY

Father, thank You for Your generous comfort and hope that can carry me through the difficulties of today. May I never become so preoccupied with the things of the present moment that I can't see how You've prepared a place for me that will overshadow the pain of today. Amen.

Worship Is a Choice

—— READ JOSHUA 24:14–27 ——

KEY VERSES

*"Now therefore revere the L*ORD*, and serve him in sincerity and in faithfulness; put away the gods that your ancestors served beyond the River and in Egypt, and serve the L*ORD*. Now if you are unwilling to serve the L*ORD*, choose this day whom you will serve, whether the gods your ancestors served in the region beyond the River or the gods of the Amorites in whose land you are living; but as for me and my household, we will serve the L*ORD*."*
JOSHUA 24:14–15 NRSV

UNDERSTAND

- How does today's passage address the spiritual danger of a divided heart?
- Why was the example of Joshua so important for the people of Israel?
- Why did Joshua give the people of Israel a choice?

APPLY

Autopilot doesn't work when it comes to your spiritual allegiance. If you let the tyranny of the urgent determine your priorities today, there's a good chance that other activities and other values will take over God's rightful place in your life. Just sliding by with the status quo of the popular culture won't serve you well.

You can start (or end) today with a simple choice about whom you will serve. The answer may not be as obvious as some think it should be because competing priorities and values can send you off course. A simple choice that sets your course for today and determines what you'll cherish above all else can prove a powerful catalyst for a life devoted to God.

If you find yourself slipping off course, consider which spiritual leaders, whether in your church or in Christian books, can help you make a better choice. Sometimes the clarity of a healthy spiritual leader or guide can make your choice of allegiance much easier to settle.

PRAY

Father, thank You for the grace and patience
You've shown me, and thank You as well
for the spiritual leaders who have helped
set a path ahead of me. May I serve You
with an undivided heart by choosing to
make You my focus for today, tomorrow,
and the days that follow. Amen.

The Source of Courage

—— READ ACTS 4:8–14 ——

KEY VERSES

*When they saw the courage of Peter and
John and realized that they were unschooled,
ordinary men, they were astonished and
they took note that these men had been with
Jesus. But since they could see the man
who had been healed standing there with
them, there was nothing they could say.*
ACTS 4:13–14 NIV

UNDERSTAND

- What gave Peter and John the courage to speak up as they did?
- What did Jesus pass on to Peter and John that helped them when confronted by the religious authorities?
- Based on the wider context of this passage, what didn't Peter and John say in this passage, and why is that significant?

APPLY

Courage doesn't just happen on its own, so if you're gearing up for a challenging situation today or if you want to be prepared for future challenges, Peter and John demonstrated a path you can follow. They learned how to speak and act courageously by being with Jesus, who had warned them on many occasions that they would face adversity. Acting courageously starts with learning from Jesus—by being with Him.

In the midst of adversity, you can also follow the example of Peter and John when they focused on the healing God had done and the benefit brought to the lame man. When you move forward in the face of criticism, you will find strength in the importance and benefit of your mission.

It's notable that Peter and John simply being with Jesus spoke volumes to others, and perhaps that is the greatest challenge for you today. The time you are with Jesus and in conversation with Him throughout your day, even if you're driving around town or working on a project at home, will produce unmistakable fruit.

PRAY

Jesus, help me to slow down and to take notice of You throughout my day. I ask for Your wisdom and power so that I can see those in need around me and then intervene for their benefit. May I always do what is right through the courage You provide. Amen.

The Keys to Continual Worship

—— READ PSALM 105:1–7 ——

KEY VERSES

Give thanks to the LORD, call upon His name;
make His deeds known among the peoples.
Sing to Him, sing praises to Him; tell of all His
wonders. Boast in His holy name; may the heart
of those who seek the LORD be joyful. Seek the
LORD and His strength; seek His face continually.
PSALM 105:1–4 NASB

UNDERSTAND

+ Which practices mentioned in today's psalm (give thanks to the Lord, make His deeds known, sing to Him, etc.) are the most natural for you to practice? How can you invest more time today in the ones that are a stretch for you?

+ What does seeking the Lord's face look like in your life? What are some ways you could make this practice something you do "continually"?

+ How could seeking the Lord lead to a joyful heart?

APPLY

Thanksgiving and singing have long been essential aspects of worship that will help you focus on the blessings God has given you—and to offer praise to God for His goodness and generosity. Singing praise of God could be in the form of a hymn, a praise song, a chant, or simply reciting a psalm to a simple melody. These practices can draw your attention away from the distractions of today and shift your gaze to God's presence.

Yet there are many other ways to offer praise to God today. As you grow in your awareness of God's goodness in your life and the ways His power has been at work in you and in others, your worship can spill over into boasting to others about God's goodness. You could say that what is often classified as "missionary" or "evangelistic" work gets merged with the practices of praise and thanksgiving.

While there are private elements to your worship, your praises for God shouldn't be limited to your own mind or prayer journal. As you seek God continually and grow in your awareness of Him, your blessings are the very things to talk about with others.

PRAY

Thank You, Father, for revealing Yourself to me this day and for being present in these quiet moments of study and prayer before You. Help me to recognize the many ways You've blessed me, and help me to take delight in boasting of Your goodness before others. Amen.

Your Primary Mission

—— READ 2 TIMOTHY 2:1–13 ——

KEY VERSES

*Share in suffering like a good soldier of
Christ Jesus. No one serving in the army gets
entangled in everyday affairs; the soldier's
aim is to please the enlisting officer. And
in the case of an athlete, no one is crowned
without competing according to the rules.*
2 TIMOTHY 2:3–5 NRSV

UNDERSTAND

+ How did Paul's mission to reach more people
  with the Gospel inform his view of suffering
  and hardship?
+ How can comparing your commitment to Christ
  with the commitment of a soldier to a command-
  ing officer help you think about your priorities
  today?
+ In what ways can comparing the Christian life
  to an athletic competition help you think about
  setting goals and enduring difficulty?

APPLY

You have a holy calling: to participate in the new
life of Christ and to share that life with others. Just
as Timothy had to be resourceful and determined in
passing that message along and enduring suffering,
you should think about the ways that God's message will be a part of your day. There are plenty

of things to juggle each day, but as a soldier who serves Christ, you should never allow the life of God to be lost in the shuffle.

Perhaps a key word from today's scripture verses to consider is *entangled*. You can't avoid being involved in the affairs of this life, and everyone has basic needs to meet, but when are you entangled in something that isn't your concern? When something ties you up to the point that you can't find time to share the life of God with others, then you will know you'll need to make adjustments.

To be certain, there are endless entanglements. There are sports teams, political parties, technology designers, app makers, and entertainers all vying for your attention. Your commitment to Christ is a calling to be involved in His new life without becoming entangled in the distractions of today.

PRAY

Jesus, thank You for including me in Your new life and for giving me the promise of overcoming suffering and death as I will one day be raised with You. Help me to see the entanglements that have kept me from serving You by sharing Your Gospel message with others. Help me to avoid distractions from my primary mission in this life. Amen.

Find Hope in the Impossible

───── READ ISAIAH 40:21–31 ─────

KEY VERSES

*Do you not know? Have you not heard? The
Lord is the everlasting God, the Creator of
the ends of the earth. He will not grow tired
or weary, and his understanding no one
can fathom. He gives strength to the weary
and increases the power of the weak. Even
youths grow tired and weary, and young
men stumble and fall; but those who hope
in the Lord will renew their strength.*
ISAIAH 40:28–31 NIV

UNDERSTAND

+ What did the people of Israel know of God
  after the tragedy of the exile and the promise
  of being restored to the land? What did they
  still need to learn?
+ Why does today's passage compare the everlasting power of God the Creator with the fleeting
  power of earthly authorities and government?
+ How is the promise to those who "hope in the
  Lord" counterintuitive to how some think of
  waiting?

APPLY

Waiting well often involves letting go of your expectations for a desired resolution delivered when you
want it. You may feel weary in a season of waiting,

but you have an everlasting resource. God, who created the heavens and outlasts every person in power and authority, seeks those who will wait, who can look ahead in faith.

Letting go of your plans and hopes doesn't feel great. You may be in a situation where you want to know that things will get better right away. But hope in God doesn't always work like that—even if God promises to renew your strength as you wait.

Just as Israel had to look to God in faith despite the seemingly impossible odds of the exile and the power of its captors, you may need to find hope in God while facing the impossible. What you know of God and His power will go a long way in determining how long you can wait and whether your hope in God will sustain you.

PRAY

I praise You, Lord, for being mighty and all-powerful. You have created all things on earth, and nothing is outside Your influence. I ask for Your mercy and healing in the places of suffering and grief in my life and in the lives of those around me. May I find hope in Your everlasting promises and renewal in Your loving presence. Amen.

Finding Hope When
the Worst Happens

—— READ GENESIS 39:10–23 ——

KEY VERSES

> *But the LORD was with Joseph in the prison
> and showed him his faithful love. And the
> LORD made Joseph a favorite with the prison
> warden. Before long, the warden put Joseph
> in charge of all the other prisoners and over
> everything that happened in the prison.*
> GENESIS 39:21–22 NLT

UNDERSTAND

- How did Joseph respond to the false accusation against him?
- Joseph certainly didn't look very blessed when he ended up in prison. How does this story challenge assumptions today about God's blessings?
- What does this passage teach about faithfulness and obedience to God?

APPLY

There's a good chance that you haven't been treated as unfairly as Joseph was, but small and large slights and mistreatments are bound to happen. Joseph's story suggests that even under the threat of a false accusation or unjust judgment against you, God will remain with you and even continue to bless you.

This calls for humility, as you will certainly

sometimes need to swallow the bitter medicine of injustice. Yet, if you trust in God, you will find that He can work with even the least desirable raw materials. What can be worse than being locked away in an ancient prison?

Even if there is pain and discomfort today in what you endure, you also can't imagine how God will shape and form you for future service to others. The worst thing that happens to you may be the key to unlocking what God has destined you to accomplish.

PRAY

Lord, thank You for the many models of Your faithfulness and love to those who have suffered unfairly. May I seek You in faith and hope without demanding specific outcomes as the sure sign of Your blessing. May I see each challenge as an opportunity to be shaped and formed into Your servant who is ready to serve others. Amen.

Trust in God, Not in
Your Own Power

—— READ MATTHEW 26:47–56 ——

KEY VERSES

*Then Jesus said to him, "Put your sword back
into its place; for all who take the sword will
perish by the sword. Do you think that I cannot
appeal to my Father, and he will at once send
me more than twelve legions of angels?"*

MATTHEW 26:52–53 NRSV

UNDERSTAND

- ♦ Why did Jesus hold back on the legions of angels
  God could have sent to rescue Him?
- ♦ What did Peter need to learn about relying on
  violence to advance God's cause?
- ♦ How does this passage help you understand
  God's power and restraint in using that power?

APPLY

Even though Peter had spent three years with Jesus,
his response to the men who had come to arrest his
Lord showed that he still had a lot to learn about
Jesus, the power of God, and the place of force in
advancing God's cause. It's simple enough to understand that God's kingdom can't be advanced by the
edge of a sword, but the deeper meaning of Jesus'
teaching about living by the sword and dying by
the sword is that mere human effort can't do what

He came to earth to accomplish.

Jesus asks you to trust God today with even the most challenging moments of your life and to know that He will have the final say one day as the all-powerful Judge. Your own power is limited, and the consequence of relying on your own strength and efforts may be far worse than you can imagine.

God is both merciful and all-powerful, but our fallen human nature can tempt us to believe that we need to depend on our own power and might. Yet even when life proves daunting, we can rest in the presence of a God who is never overwhelmed or overpowered.

PRAY

Jesus, thank You for Your power and patience, both of which guide our world and give many an opportunity to know You personally. May I imitate Your mercy and restraint with others while also trusting in Your all-powerful rule over the earth. Amen.

Guidelines for Great Leadership

—— READ 2 TIMOTHY 2:15–26 ——

KEY VERSES

> *Work hard so you can present yourself to God and receive his approval. Be a good worker, one who does not need to be ashamed and who correctly explains the word of truth. Avoid worthless, foolish talk that only leads to more godless behavior.*
> 2 TIMOTHY 2:15–16 NLT

UNDERSTAND

- Timothy had to keep himself prepared for God's work. How are obedience and purity key parts of being ready to do that work?
- How did the idea of presenting himself to God influence the way Timothy pursued his ministry?
- What is the danger of foolish talk for a Christian leader like Timothy?

APPLY

The Bible holds church leaders to higher standards. Whether you are a leader or simply trying to discern whether a leader is reliable enough to follow, today's passage is instructive because it tells us to look for leaders—and to be leaders—who don't engage in worthless arguments, foolish talk, or vain quarrels. Such actions undermine both leaders' and followers' work in spreading the Gospel.

Ideal leaders—those who can help unlock the

wider potential of the church to serve God and others—are those who patiently and gently instruct others. They lead and teach even the most difficult and argumentative of people with kindness and humility that doesn't alienate them and still hopes for their redemption.

Leaders who allow themselves to become distracted or combative most often cause those who follow them to also become distracted and combative. But those who follow the advice Paul gave to Timothy benefit both individuals and their communities simply because they are focused on opportunities for growth and on the worthiest of goals.

PRAY

Jesus, send Your church leaders who are humble servants and capable teachers who can discern between what is worthwhile and what is a distraction. May these leaders help me to remain true to Your teachings and help draw me nearer to You. Help me to be that kind of leader. Amen.

Trust in God Alone

———— READ PSALM 33:13–22 ————

KEY VERSES

*A horse is a false hope for victory; nor does
it rescue anyone by its great strength. Behold,
the eye of the LORD is on those who fear Him,
on those who wait for His faithfulness.*
PSALM 33:17–18 NASB

UNDERSTAND

+ What does today's passage tell us about those
  who depend on something other than God for
  their strength and victory?
+ How does the writer of Psalm 33 offer assurance
  to those who wait on the Lord?
+ Today's scripture reading begins with God
  looking down from heaven on all of humanity
  (v. 13). How does that image shape the promises
  that follow?

APPLY

Consider for a moment the sources of stress, uncertainty, and fear in your life. Look at the areas where you wish you had more control and influence. Consider how you go about trying to solve or address these challenges each day.

There are many people, organizations, possessions, and financial resources on which you rely and place your trust today to solve your problems. But today's psalm makes God's place in this world unmistakable and supreme over everything else. It guarantees that even the best manmade solutions, though they may work for a time, will eventually let you down.

The only sure bet is the God who looks down from heaven and sees everything unfolding on earth below. You may need to wait a while to see your hope in God fulfilled, but there is certainly no safer bet than trusting in God.

PRAY

Thank You, Lord, for Your deep love and concern for Your people. You hear my cries when I call out to You, and You promise to care for me in difficult times. May I leave behind my hope in anything else that promises security and learn to wait patiently for Your help. Amen.

God Longs for Your Return

—— READ ZECHARIAH 1:1–6 ——

KEY VERSES

> *"Therefore tell the people: This is what the* LORD *Almighty says: 'Return to me,' declares the* LORD *Almighty, 'and I will return to you,' says the* LORD *Almighty. Do not be like your ancestors, to whom the earlier prophets proclaimed: This is what the* LORD *Almighty says: 'Turn from your evil ways and your evil practices.' But they would not listen or pay attention to me, declares the* LORD*."*
>
> ZECHARIAH 1:3–4 NIV

UNDERSTAND

* What is the significance of this passage in light of God's people being exiled?
* What does God want His people to learn from past generations?
* Why is it so important for the people to make the first step toward returning to God?

APPLY

Take a moment today to think about how your failures or bad life choices have come between yourself and God. These could be in your distant past, or they could have happened yesterday. Think of the burdens you have carried that have led to feelings of shame and isolation from God.

Much like God sought out Adam and Eve hiding

in the garden, he sought out the people of Judah while they were in exile in Babylon. He reaches out to you today in the same way. The choice you make to return to God is all that you need to do to start again.

God is ready and willing to extend forgiveness and restoration to you, and He invites you to take that first step by returning to Him. Past generations have missed out on God's mercy and offer of restoration, but you have an opportunity today to reunite yourself with a merciful and kind God who longs for your return.

PRAY

*Thank You, Lord, that Your mercy and
forgiveness overcome my greatest failures
and deepest shame. Help me to learn
from the mistakes of past generations
who rejected Your mercy. May I make a
definitive choice to return to You with an
open heart and a teachable mind. Amen.*

Obedience Requires Risk

—— READ PSALM 106:24–31 ——

KEY VERSES

*The people refused to enter the pleasant
land, for they wouldn't believe his promise
to care for them. Instead, they grumbled in
their tents and refused to obey the Lord.*
PSALM 106:24–25 NLT

UNDERSTAND

- If the Promised Land was such a "pleasant" place, why did the Israelites resist entering the land?
- How did the Israelites' thoughts about God prompt them to grumble?
- What does this passage suggest about the challenges of obeying God's commands?

APPLY

God can lead you on many paths toward blessings and joy, but it's often likely that the paths toward those blessings and joy will be difficult—and some may even appear dangerous. Receiving God's blessings often requires risk and sacrifice, and it may mean leaving the comfort of what you know behind and reaching out for His next new thing with open hands.

When you resist the high risks and high rewards of seeking God's blessings, you place yourself in opposition to Him. The more you grumble and complain against God's direction in your life, the more you alienate yourself from Him.

In the case of the Israelites in the wilderness, it took the courageous intervention of the priest Phinehas going against the trends of the time. Such advocates and spiritual guides will be essential for your own perseverance. Look for people who are both dedicated to God's will and capable of speaking the truth courageously.

PRAY

Thank You, Lord, for Your kindness to provide for Your people, just as You once led Your people to the Promised Land. May I look to You in faith and take courage to obey Your commands. The risks are numerous, but reaching Your blessings is well worth the challenge. Amen.

Joy and Mourning Can Coexist

———— READ EZRA 3:8–13 ————

KEY VERSES

> *When the builders laid the foundation of*
> *the temple of the LORD, the priests in their*
> *vestments were stationed to praise the*
> *LORD with trumpets, and the Levites, the*
> *sons of Asaph, with cymbals, according to*
> *the directions of King David of Israel; and*
> *they sang responsively, praising and giving*
> *thanks to the LORD, "For he is good, for his*
> *steadfast love endures forever toward Israel."*
> EZRA 3:10–11 NRSV

UNDERSTAND

* What was the significance of rebuilding the temple after the people began returning from the Babylonian exile?
* What do you think it was like to sing praises to God while standing around the rubble of the former temple and former city walls?
* Why do you think it was so important for the people to praise God at the beginning of the temple work?

APPLY

Ezra records that the people shouted both for joy and in mourning when they saw the second temple's foundation. Mourning and joy often go together— like when a joyous family gathering reminds you of a lost loved one. . .or when the start of a new venture also means the end of a previous task that felt like the perfect fit. You can both thank God and mourn your losses at the same time—in fact, your spiritual and emotional health may depend on it!

A simple examination of what you're thankful for and what's causing you to struggle can help you take stock of the emotions at play in the present moment. Perhaps you're in a season of thankfulness and healing, seeing many struggles come to a happy resolution.

Then again, you may be facing a lot of pain and uncertainty, which makes it hard to rejoice. You can still mourn what has been lost while appreciating the good things you have in the present. In fact, the longer you deny the pain that weighs on your mind, the harder it will be to fully enjoy the good things coming in your life.

PRAY

Thank You, Lord, that You have compassion on those who mourn and that You want to turn our mourning into gladness. I ask for comfort for my own sorrow—and for the sorrows of others—and thank You for Your provision for those who seek You with thankful hearts. Amen.

Celebrating God's Power and Goodness

——— READ EXODUS 15:1-11 ———

KEY VERSES

*Then Moses and the Israelites sang this song
to the LORD: "I will sing to the LORD, for
he is highly exalted. Both horse and driver
he has hurled into the sea. The LORD is my
strength and my defense; he has become my
salvation. He is my God, and I will praise
him, my father's God, and I will exalt him."*
EXODUS 15:1-2 NIV

UNDERSTAND

- What emotions do you think the Israelites felt
  after seeing God sweep away the Egyptian army
  in the sea?
- What details about God are mentioned in today's
  scripture reading?
- How did their view of God change after being
  delivered from slavery in Egypt and from the
  Egyptian soldiers on the far side of the sea?

APPLY

There are moments in life when God shows up in
ways that seem more obvious and apparent than
others. Although you may have endured long seasons
of distance from God, a sudden revelation of His
power pulls back the veil between God and you.

These are moments to celebrate and to remember.

A moment of revelation or awareness of God may not last forever. The Israelites' challenging years of slavery were soon followed by wandering in the wilderness. Their disobedience and fear prevented them from fully entering into God's rest in a new land.

One way to guard your heart in preparation for the challenging times is to praise God for the good things He has done. Such moments of praise and thanksgiving can make it easier to remember how the Lord has acted in your favor and helps you remain grounded when life becomes difficult. Celebration isn't a frivolous use of your time. It's a vital part of your worship and faith.

PRAY

Thank You, Lord, for the ways You have provided and cared for Your people throughout the years—and for the ways You have provided and cared for me. Today I will remember and rejoice in Your provision and kindness toward me, trusting that You will never fail me. Amen.

Handling Compromise

READ 1 KINGS 11:1-13

KEY VERSES

> *In Solomon's old age, they turned his heart to worship other gods instead of being completely faithful to the LORD his God, as his father, David, had been. Solomon worshiped Ashtoreth, the goddess of the Sidonians, and Molech, the detestable god of the Ammonites.*
> 1 KINGS 11:4–5 NLT

UNDERSTAND

- How do you think Solomon justified marrying women who worshipped false gods? Why did he tolerate their worship of these deities?
- How did the writer of 1 Kings characterize Solomon's faithfulness—or lack of faithfulness—to the Lord?
- What do the consequences of Solomon's unfaithfulness suggest about the high cost of compromise?

APPLY

Compromise has a way of sneaking up on a man— one ungodly decision here, one corner cut there— and in time we can find ourselves living a life of repeated compromise over what God tells us is right. Any of us can find ourselves making excuses for our compromise, and we may even convince others that we are right or justified in compromising. But compromising our faithfulness to God will always wear us down over time, and the results may be far worse than we ever could have imagined or intended at the outset.

Complete, uncompromising faithfulness to God may feel like a high standard to hold. It's a commitment to examine yourself and finding areas of compromise in your life. When you find areas of compromise, it's best that you confess them to God and ask Him to help you to do better.

You have an opportunity today to examine your life to ensure that you are completely faithful and committed to the Lord. If you've failed, you're in good company. God will be gracious to forgive you, just as He has forgiven so many of His people who have repented for falling into compromise. If you return to God, He will certainly return to you.

PRAY

Thank You, Lord, for Your mercy and forgiveness that lift me up whenever I fail. May You examine my heart and expose any places that are divided or not given wholly to You so that I can serve You and Your people with a single-minded commitment all the days of my life. Amen.

God Hears the Prayers of the Destitute

—— READ PSALM 102:12–22 ——

KEY VERSES

*For the Lord will build up Zion; he will appear
in his glory. He will regard the prayer of the
destitute, and will not despise their prayer. Let
this be recorded for a generation to come, so
that a people yet unborn may praise the Lord.*
PSALM 102:16–18, NRSV

UNDERSTAND

* How does Psalm 102 consider the praise and worship of today in light of the worship of future generations?
* As the people of Israel suffered the tragedy of exile, how did they find hope in the Lord?
* What is the significance of the Lord hearing the groans of prisoners and those condemned to die?

APPLY

Each day you are surrounded by people who are suffering immensely today or who bear the wounds from past trauma. You may even be among them. Some are trapped in a mental prison of depression from past trauma, and some are dealing with real limitations that hold them back from personal freedom. But the Lord is aware of people's cries for relief and wants to have compassion on them.

Today's psalm encourages us to pray to God for relief—for ourselves or for others who are suffering. And when God acts on our behalf, we will be able to praise Him for what He has done for us.

Suffering may be temporary, but the Lord is enthroned in heaven forever. There is no limit to His power and compassion. One day God will appear in glory to right the wrongs of today. In the meantime, we should keep ourselves in a constant state of prayer as we wait for Him to act.

PRAY

Lord, You see my suffering and the suffering of others, and You desire to bring justice and relief to all who suffer. Help me to wait patiently for You, placing my faith in Your everlasting power and the hope that You will one day return to earth to rule. Amen.

Rewards for Godly Living

—— READ MATTHEW 5:1-11 ——

KEY VERSES

*"Blessed are the meek, for they will inherit
the earth. Blessed are those who hunger
and thirst for righteousness, for they will
be filled. Blessed are the merciful, for
they will be shown mercy. Blessed are the
pure in heart, for they will see God."*
MATTHEW 5:5-8 NIV

UNDERSTAND

+ Why does Jesus make such an amazing promise
  to those who are "meek"?
+ Why is mercy such an important quality in the
  Beatitudes?
+ Why is purity of heart so instrumental in seeing
  God? What did Jesus mean when He said the
  pure in heart will "see God"?

APPLY

The Beatitudes—Jesus' statements of blessings
found in today's scripture reading—suggest a way
of living that is in opposition to the "wisdom" of
the world today. But these are Jesus' promises of
joy and fulfillment for those who orient their lives
and thinking according to God's wisdom. This is
Jesus' invitation to keep ourselves in the right perspective so that we can be fully present for God
and for others.

Some of these promises may come to fruition in the present, and some may be fulfilled when we are in the very presence of God. Either way, we can count on Him to keep these and every other promise He has made. He has said it, and He will do it!

Yet even with so many promises that will be fulfilled one day, the wisdom of Jesus remains especially true for you today. If you hope to receive mercy, then be merciful toward others. If you want things to be made right in this life, then you need to crave it like it's the food that sustains you. And as you align your desires with God's will, Jesus promises that you will find fulfillment.

PRAY

Jesus, help me to see the world through Your eyes and to value what You value. May I look ahead to the rewards You have promised me, and may I take actions that bring benefit to those around me. I ask that Your power and influence in my life would lead me to a pure heart and a greater awareness of You. Amen.

Remember God's Faithfulness

—— READ DEUTERONOMY 11:1–12 ——

KEY VERSES

> *Observe therefore all the commands I am*
> *giving you today, so that you may have*
> *the strength to go in and take over the*
> *land that you are crossing the Jordan to*
> *possess, and so that you may live long in*
> *the land the LORD swore to your ancestors*
> *to give to them and their descendants,*
> *a land flowing with milk and honey.*
> DEUTERONOMY 11:8–9 NIV

UNDERSTAND

+ Why was obedience so important for the Israelites as they entered the land God promised
  to them?
+ God promised the land to the people of Israel
  and their descendants. Why did He remind them
  of this promise at this moment?
+ How could it help the people of Israel to be
  reminded of how God had delivered them from
  the armies of Egypt in the past?

APPLY

Consider the challenges you are facing today or this
week—or the worries weighing on your mind. Take
notice of them and how they are impacting you.
As you see these challenges with clarity, you can
also look at the ways God has been with you, the

people in your family, or those in your immediate circles through difficult times.

Remembering God's past faithfulness as you think about your present challenges will help you realize both the stakes of your day and the hope He offers. Most importantly, obedience is a key part of remaining close to God throughout today and the rest of your week.

As you listen to God's commands and act obediently, you'll have the intimacy and access to Him you need to thrive in your difficulties. Obedience ensures that you see your life on God's terms and are prepared to depend on Him rather than your own resources or plans. Drawing near to God in obedience will ensure that He is already near when you are in need.

PRAY

Thank You, Lord, for the ways You've been present for Your people, providing for their needs and delivering them from trouble. May I live today with an awareness of Your power and ability to save. And may my awareness of You help me to live in faithful obedience. Amen.

Encouragement to Yield to God's Plans

—— READ 1 SAMUEL 23:13–24 ——

KEY VERSES

Jonathan went to find David and encouraged him to stay strong in his faith in God. "Don't be afraid," Jonathan reassured him. "My father will never find you! You are going to be the king of Israel, and I will be next to you, as my father, Saul, is well aware."
1 SAMUEL 23:16–17 NLT

UNDERSTAND

- What does it say about Jonathan's faith in God that he gave up his rightful place as the king of Israel after Saul's death?
- Why did David need encouragement from Jonathan while King Saul was trying to kill him?
- What is the benefit of making a solemn pact before God with another person?

APPLY

When someone reads God's promises in scripture, but they don't seem to make sense in light of their current circumstances, it may feel like they are on the ropes in their life of faith. In a situation where nothing seems to be going right or when someone feels like God has abandoned them, a timely word of encouragement can make the difference.

Faith and encouragement may require looking for things that are quite different from present circumstances. You may have to set aside your desires or how you think things should be in order to fully embrace the good things God has planned for those in need of encouragement.

Today, keep an eye out for those who are faltering or discouraged in their faith, and then consider how you can help them trust in God. You may be the person who keeps them on track to one day accomplish great things for God.

PRAY

Help me, Lord, to see the people around me who are discouraged, struggling with their faith, or facing adversity and uncertainty. May I support them with encouragement and intercession when they are most in need of compassionate, considerate assistance. Amen.

God Is Greater Than Any Challenge You Face

—— READ 2 CHRONICLES 32:1–8 ——

KEY VERSES

> *"Be strong and courageous, do not fear or be dismayed because of the king of Assyria nor because of all the horde that is with him; for the One with us is greater than the one with him. With him is only an arm of flesh, but with us is the LORD our God to help us and to fight our battles." And the people relied on the words of Hezekiah king of Judah.*
> 2 CHRONICLES 32:7–8 NASB

UNDERSTAND

- Hezekiah had been faithful to God before the Assyrian invasion of the land. Why did the author of Chronicles mention this detail at the start of today's reading?
- How did Hezekiah contrast the power of God with the power of the king of Assyria?
- What does this passage say about spiritual leadership and the impact a leader's encouraging words can have on the faith of others?

APPLY

There's a good chance that you're facing some kind of challenge today. You may feel the weight of a difficult relationship, the uncertainty of a job, or the weary grind of many responsibilities stacked on top of each other. If there is no one in your life to encourage you and lift you up, those challenges can feel all-consuming, even crushing.

Today's scripture reading encourages you to shift your focus from your own difficulties to God's extensive power and resources, which can be unleashed in your life—if only you turn toward Him in faith. King Hezekiah and the people of Judah were an example of this truth. They had seen the Assyrians destroy one nation after another, but they took timely action and trusted in God to do the rest.

You may need to make some big, uncomfortable changes to your life to overcome the challenges before you. But the good news is that God is all-powerful and willing to remain with you through the highs and lows of today. If you remain in God, He will remain with you.

PRAY

Lord, You know better than I do what my challenges are and how I can best overcome them. Thank You for being near Your people in their times of challenge and struggle. May Your power be manifested on my behalf so that I am safe in Your presence. Amen.

God's Love Will Lead You

———— READ PSALM 5:1-8 ————

KEY VERSES

But I, through the abundance of your steadfast love, will enter your house, I will bow down toward your holy temple in awe of you. Lead me, O LORD, in your righteousness because of my enemies; make your way straight before me.
PSALM 5:7-8 NRSV

UNDERSTAND

- Why was it so important for David, the writer of Psalm 5, to rely on the Lord's guidance for a straight path forward?
- According to Psalm 5, on what basis can we approach God's temple in worship? How is someone declared "worthy" before God?
- This psalm contrasts those who delight in evil, who are deceitful, and who lie with those who rise early to make their requests known to God. How are these two approaches to problem-solving most different?

APPLY

There are two paths you can travel today. One is a path of self-reliance that can sometimes turn into lying and cheating to get ahead; the other, a path that starts every day with requests to God and a complete reliance on Him to set a clear path for you.

Today's scripture reading assures us that God is not far from us when we are committed to His truth. If you fail to commit yourself to God's truth, you'll miss out on the opportunity to boldly step into His presence, which is where we receive mercy and guidance.

You don't have to worry today about finding the right path forward, simply because God, in His great love, will lead you—as long as you are open to His leading. God's presence will be with you, and that will be enough. Any other source of guidance or wisdom will let you down and lead you to a dead end, but that will never happen when you follow God's path for you.

PRAY

Thank You, Lord, for Your love, grace, and mercy—all of which You promise will meet me in my weakness and uncertainty today. May I find the time at the start of each day to share my requests with You and then trust that You will guide me in the correct path forward. Amen.

Hope in God after Failure

—— READ PSALM 39:7–13 ——

KEY VERSES

> *And now, Lord, for what do I wait?*
> *My hope is in You. Save me from all*
> *my wrongdoings; Do not make me an*
> *object of reproach for the foolish.*
> PSALM 39:7–8 NASB

UNDERSTAND

- Psalm 39 suggests that God has disciplined David the psalmist after a season of disobedience. How does that discipline coexist with grace and forgiveness?
- What else could David have waited for instead of God?
- How could this season of waiting become derailed? How could it become beneficial and fruitful?

APPLY

Failure is a part of life, and everyone has willfully disobeyed God at certain moments. Psalm 39 notes an especially lonely and serious moment when the consequences of sin offer a painful but useful reminder of the fragility of mankind and the brief nature of life. It shows us that life is too short to waste on rebellion against God, for the suffering that comes from rebellion will drain your enjoyment quickly.

Today's scripture reading poses an important question: Are you willing to humble yourself before God in order to be restored?

Waiting on God sometimes means bearing the full brunt of the consequences of your actions—and even His hand of discipline. Adding to the challenge is the fact that an answer from God may not be forthcoming on your timetable, and the path to restoration may be difficult and uncomfortable. Yet no other source of hope will lift you from despair over your own failure like God.

PRAY

Help me, Lord, to recognize my failures and compromises so that I can confess them and be restored. May I remain near to You and aware that each careless sin can bring me more pain than I could ever intend or imagine. Help me to wait patiently for You and You alone. Amen.

Jesus Came to Heal

—— READ LUKE 5:27–39 ——

KEY VERSES

> *But the Pharisees and the teachers*
> *of the law who belonged to their sect*
> *complained to his disciples, "Why do*
> *you eat and drink with tax collectors*
> *and sinners?" Jesus answered them, "It*
> *is not the healthy who need a doctor,*
> *but the sick. I have not come to call the*
> *righteous, but sinners to repentance."*
>
> LUKE 5:30–32 NIV

UNDERSTAND

- What is the difference between the "job description" for the Pharisees and the teachers of the law and the one Jesus adopted for Himself?
- How can we liken Jesus' earthly ministry to the work of a physician?
- What was Jesus accomplishing by eating and drinking with notorious "sinners"?

APPLY

Pause for a moment and consider how you see God. Do you see Him as a harsh judge who is eager to sentence you for your sins or as a heavenly doctor who is dedicated to your healing and restoration?

When you feel shame over something, maybe to the point where you feel unworthy of God, remember that Jesus has come to heal you and make you worthy. You can come to Jesus as you would a doctor—with complete honesty about what is wrong, not hiding anything. When you do, you'll find hope that Jesus will heal the parts of you that never seem to be sorted out.

When Jesus heals you and forgives you, He also gives you the liberating calling of bringing others to Him for healing others as well. You don't have to worry about who others might see as worthy and unworthy. You only need to share the joyful news that Jesus has come to heal the sick and sinners— and that there is hope in repentance.

PRAY

Thank You, Jesus, for coming to heal me and restore me so that I no longer need to live in shame or struggle to obey You. May I enjoy the liberty and freedom that comes from knowing You, and may I share that healing and hope with those I meet today. Amen.

Ponder Your Life's Direction

———— READ PSALM 119:57–72 ————

KEY VERSES

Lord, you are mine! I promise to obey
your words! With all my heart I want your
blessings. Be merciful as you promised.
I pondered the direction of my life, and I
turned to follow your laws. I will hurry,
without delay, to obey your commands.

PSALM 119:57–60 NLT

UNDERSTAND

+ What is the benefit of making a promise of obedience to God?
+ Why is it important to ponder the direction of your life? How did this pondering help the writer of today's scripture reading?
+ Why is the writer of today's key verses in a hurry to obey God's commands without delay?

APPLY

Taking time to really think about the direction of your life can yield a lot of insights and wisdom that lead to better decisions and choices each day. By viewing the big picture of your life and where you hope to end up, you can ensure that your choices line up with your goals—and with God's goals for you.

Obedience to God requires intention and determination to rely on God's power and hold on to His promises. If you don't know what God has promised you, you won't know what you can ask of Him or how you can rely on Him. The more you learn about God's promises, the more faith you can put in Him—and the less pressure you'll put on yourself.

Don't delay in obedience to God, and don't neglect your spiritual life. If you're running counter to God's Spirit and His purposes, you'll develop habits and patterns that make it harder to receive His blessings.

PRAY

Lord, help me to see the larger picture of disobedience and obedience so that I can keep in step with Your Spirit and stay within the direction of Your will. Amen.

Free to Honor and Serve Others

──── READ 1 PETER 2:11-25 ────

KEY VERSES

*For it is God's will that by doing right you
should silence the ignorance of the foolish.
As servants of God, live as free people, yet do
not use your freedom as a pretext for evil.*
1 PETER 2:15-16 NRSV

UNDERSTAND

+ It's implied in today's key verses that doing the
  right thing isn't necessarily the natural response
  to the ignorance of the foolish. What do you
  think Peter had in mind when he set up this
  contrast?
+ How does living in "freedom" make Christians
  more likely to be servants of God and others?
+ What are some ways that Peter expected Christians to honor everyone?

APPLY

You will likely experience times when others won't
fully understand you or give you the benefit of a
doubt. Others may even malign you at times. Yet
the apostle Peter, who had a fiery temper at one
point in his life, suggested that the best response
is to simply do what's right. He even added that
you are free to honor everyone, even when you
are mistreated.

Your restraint when you are mistreated is in keeping with God's will and ultimately silences those who are most provocative. That isn't an easy task in the heat of the moment, but if reaching resolutions matters to you, then Peter's advice is sound.

Tied in with this calling to respond with grace to insults and misunderstandings is the greater mission to use your freedom in Christ well. Being free from the law doesn't mean anything goes. It's a greater responsibility to remain in Christ and to be even more aware of others. How you live before them will shape how they view Jesus, and if His life is present in you, then you'll help them see God's work with clarity.

PRAY

> *Thank You, Jesus, that You have set me free*
> *to be Your servant, a servant who is free*
> *to love others. When I am misunderstood*
> *or treated unfairly, help me to remember*
> *how You were mistreated and still showed*
> *mercy so that I can honor everyone and*
> *respond with Your same grace. Amen.*

God Knows What You Can Handle

——— READ 1 KINGS 19:1–9 ———

KEY VERSES

The angel of the LORD came back a second time
and touched Elijah and said, "Get up and eat,
for the journey is too much for you." So he got
up and ate and drank. Strengthened by that
food, he traveled forty days and forty nights
until he reached Horeb, the mountain of God.
1 KINGS 19:7–8 NIV

UNDERSTAND

- Elijah felt hopeless as he fled the threats from King Ahab and Queen Jezebel. Why is it important that the angel acknowledged the journey was too much for Elijah?
- Why was a retreat into the wilderness so important for Elijah after his confrontations with the prophets of Baal and the king and queen of Israel?
- What does today's scripture reading suggest about God's approach to His people when they are suffering through seasons of discouragement?

APPLY

God knows better than you what you can handle—and when you've reached your limit, your own doubts and discouragement aren't going to scare Him away. In fact, it's when you feel most overwhelmed and burned out that God can support you the most. Yes, there are moments in life that are too much for you, but God will remain with you throughout them.

Taking a page from Elijah's story, the best step you can take when feeling overwhelmed is to retreat to a quiet, solitary place and speak honestly to God about how you're feeling. Then. . .just wait patiently. You may not hear exactly what you expect from God in that moment of retreat (remember, He gave Elijah more tasks to accomplish), but you will receive the mercy and provision you need to continue.

Your trials and struggles aren't a surprise to God. He will meet you in the pauses and solitary moments of your day to help you continue in faith and hope.

PRAY

Thank You, Lord, for Your presence and provision during difficult times. I ask that You lift me up and encourage me in the moments when I feel most overwhelmed and uncertain about what's next. May I find courage and hope in Your comforting presence. Amen.

What Is God Asking You to Do?

——— READ ISAIAH 61 ———

KEY VERSES

The Spirit of the Sovereign LORD is upon me,
for the LORD has anointed me to bring good
news to the poor. He has sent me to comfort
the brokenhearted and to proclaim that captives
will be released and prisoners will be freed. He
has sent me to tell those who mourn that the
time of the LORD's favor has come, and with it,
the day of God's anger against their enemies.
ISAIAH 61:1–2 NLT

UNDERSTAND

+ How would a message of future deliverance from a Messiah give hope to people living in exile in a foreign nation?
+ How did the idea of being "anointed" by God give greater meaning to this calling to bring God's good news to the poor, brokenhearted, and captives?
+ What do the different people groups listed in this passage reveal about God's concerns and priorities?

APPLY

Much like in the times of Isaiah and Jesus, who based His ministry on this prophetic passage, God's Spirit may be guiding you or even prompting you to take specific actions. Today you can begin to look at the people around you who may be in need or who are suffering. Does God have something specific for you to do or to say in a particular situation?

You don't have to look at serving others as a solo venture. God is with you and will lead you. There are plenty of worthy ministries you could get involved in, but you only need to concern yourself with where the Spirit has led you and where the "anointing" of God rests.

Service under God's direction isn't flashy or high profile. It's often a simple loving presence that could include providing relief to the brokenhearted, sharing God's hope with those who mourn, and setting things right with those in need of restoration. Most importantly, when God calls you to serve others, God will go with you, lead you, and empower you to do what you didn't even think possible.

PRAY

Father, thank You for the ways You've guided and empowered Your people throughout history. Lead me forward today, and give me eyes to see and ears to hear Your calling so that I can serve those in the greatest need of Your healing touch and hopeful message. Amen.

How Do You Spend Your Time?

———— READ PSALM 27:1–10 ————

KEY VERSES

One thing I have asked from the LORD, that I shall seek: that I may dwell in the house of the LORD all the days of my life, to behold the beauty of the LORD and to meditate in His temple. For on the day of trouble He will conceal me in His tabernacle; He will hide me in the secret place of His tent; He will lift me up on a rock.

PSALM 27:4–5 NASB

UNDERSTAND

- Since it wasn't possible for the people of Israel to actually live in the temple, what does this psalm mean when it says to "dwell in the house of the LORD"?
- What are the psalmist's goals as he is in the temple of the Lord?
- How does dwelling in the Lord's house change the direction of the psalmist's life? How does the psalmist benefit from these changes?

APPLY

You can "dwell" at your home, at your workplace, at a friend's house, or at a store for part of your day. But the writer of Psalm 27 adopts a broader, deeper understanding of what it means to "dwell" as he describes both *where* you spend your time and *how* you spend your time. The time you spend in worship, alone with God or in a "church" setting, can serve as a catalyst for "dwelling" with the Lord.

As a recipient of the Holy Spirit, you are indwelt by God. And so the act of dwelling with God has much more to do with your awareness and intention each day.

Where you dwell and how you spend your time will significantly impact how you weather the storms of life and the challenges that may be coming today. You'll find stability and hope when you dwell with God and trust in His presence to carry you through whatever life here on earth may bring your way.

PRAY

Thank You, Lord, for Your comforting and empowering presence. Help me to remain in You so that I can be full of faith and hope in Your power and guidance. May I stay mindful of Your promise never to leave or forsake me as the difficulties of life increase. Amen.

Where Do You Find Refuge?

———— READ PSALM 61 ————

KEY VERSES

*Hear my cry, O God; listen to my prayer.
From the end of the earth I call to you,
when my heart is faint. Lead me to the
rock that is higher than I; for you are my
refuge, a strong tower against the enemy.*

PSALM 61:1–3 NRSV

UNDERSTAND

+ What is the significance of calling out to God
  from the ends of the earth and expecting Him
  to hear your prayer?
+ What does it mean that God is the "rock" that
  is higher than you? How is that image similar
  or different from God being a strong tower?
+ Why does the psalmist ask to be led to the rock?
  Who do you think the psalmist is addressing
  with that question?

APPLY

There are many places you can turn to for help
during times of difficulty. But when you see challenges before you and trouble coming your way,
you have a ready-made refuge in the Lord. You can
approach God with confidence, knowing that He
will hear your prayers and that He will take your
well-being seriously.

But how can we cultivate that inner confidence

in our God? We can look to the stories in the promises found in scripture as well as biblical examples of God answering prayer and caring for His people. We can also draw from the experiences of fellow Christians as well as our own moments when God was present during difficult times.

The images of a high rock or strong tower may not be familiar to many today, but these things were used in scripture as illustrations of God's promise of protection and safety.

PRAY

Thank You, Father, that I am safe and secure in Your loving presence. You know my needs and hear me wherever I may pray to You. May I always find my safety and security in You, never settling for any other source of hope. Amen.

God Rewards Right Actions and Just Intentions

———— READ JEREMIAH 17:9–18 ————

KEY VERSES

"The heart is more deceitful than all else and is desperately sick; who can understand it? I, the LORD, search the heart, I test the mind, to give to each person according to his ways, according to the results of his deeds."

JEREMIAH 17:9–10 NASB

UNDERSTAND

- How does God's understanding of the human heart's deceptiveness bring assurance to you about God's justice and righteousness?
- How does the idea of the Lord understanding and searching your heart guide your thoughts about sin and obedience?
- What does the Lord's promise to reward or punish people according to their deeds imply about those who think they are sinning in secret?

APPLY

The Lord assured Jeremiah that the people around him, even those who were prospering while disobeying God, would soon receive a just reward for their actions. There is no doubt that the choices you make today to follow God may feel like sacrifices and may even lead to some tension and difficulties.

Yet the Lord will certainly make sure that your good deeds, honesty, and obedience will be rewarded.

God sees your purity of heart and intentions. Even when those around you fail to appreciate your faithfulness, God searches your heart and sees your commitments to justice and goodness. Those who act with duplicity or out of secretly selfish motives are also seen for what they are before God and will one day receive what they deserve.

It's tough to wait on God's reward in a culture immersed in instant gratification. How can you wait patiently for a reward you can't even quite imagine? You certainly don't even know when you'll be rewarded by God. The Lord invites you to take a leap of faith, trusting that your obedience and goodness today will not go to waste.

PRAY

Lord, You know my heart and mind before I can even speak. Thank You for Your mercy and compassion to forgive my sins and Your promise to reward my obedience. May I live today in dependence on You and Your provision. Amen.

Choose to Celebrate with God

──────── READ LUKE 15:11–32 ────────

KEY VERSES

"'But when this son of yours who has squandered your property with prostitutes comes home, you kill the fattened calf for him!' 'My son,' the father said, 'you are always with me, and everything I have is yours. But we had to celebrate and be glad, because this brother of yours was dead and is alive again; he was lost and is found.'"

LUKE 15:30–32 NIV

UNDERSTAND

- ♦ How do people typically respond when others are shown mercy and forgiveness?
- ♦ Why did the father in today's scripture reading assure his son who remained at home that everything he has also belongs to him?
- ♦ Why was celebrating so important at a time when some may expect punishment and discipline?

APPLY

God's mercy is almost always larger and more extensive than people expect. Whether you feel that you've gone past the point of no return or that you've lived in meticulous obedience for as long as you can remember, there is a place for you in today's reading.

God's mercy will always win when someone repents of sin, but the welcome party can take on a sour note to those who reject God's mercy. There is a party you are invited to join either as the recipient of God's mercy or as a member of the party sharing in the joy of restoration. While the sulking son in the parable of the lost son refused to join the party because of what had happened in the past, God (like the father in this story) invites everyone to look forward to the future together.

The celebration of repentance doesn't minimize or gloss over sin. This party recognizes the seriousness of the sin, but it also celebrates the movement from death into life. This is truly cause for great celebration.

PRAY

Thank You, Father, for Your mercy and kindness—for Your promises I can always return to You and celebrate in Your mercy and hope of renewal. May I share Your grace and mercy with others who are also in need of restoration and a new chance to live in obedience to You. Amen.

God Heals Our Pain

—— READ ISAIAH 53:1–12 ——

KEY VERSES

He was despised and rejected—a man of sorrows, acquainted with deepest grief. We turned our backs on him and looked the other way. He was despised, and we did not care. Yet it was our weaknesses he carried; it was our sorrows that weighed him down.

ISAIAH 53:3–4 NLT

UNDERSTAND

- ♦ Why is it so significant that God's Servant (Christ) wasn't beautiful or attractive?
- ♦ What does it mean to you that God's Servant was a man of sorrows who was acquainted with deepest grief?
- ♦ What is the result of God carrying our weaknesses and our sorrows?

APPLY

God's starting point with His people is often their pain and suffering, as He seeks out those who are overlooked, neglected, and sorrowful so that they can be restored. Even God's own approach to our salvation came through the Man of Sorrows who bore the sin, sadness, and weakness of the world.

This is a major difference from the approach of our world today, where suffering is avoided, overlooked, and even actively hidden. Pastors who promise blessings and prosperity have no trouble drawing a crowd, but the dark side of such approaches is an inability to speak into the pain and loss that is certain to come in this world.

Jesus bore your grief and sadness and offers the hope of renewal and restoration. That hope isn't an empty promise with glamour and comfort. Jesus went through the path of suffering and transformed it. You can bring your pain to God today and trust that you aren't bearing it alone. That pain is right where God plans to be. And if you see others who are suffering, remember that God is near to them as well, and you can imitate God's example by sharing in their sorrow. One day your joy will be all the greater when God's restoration comes.

PRAY

Help me, Father, to see my suffering as an opportunity to draw near to You and to remember that You see my sorrow. May I acknowledge my pain and remain aware of those enduring grief and loss so that I can imitate the example of Jesus. Amen.

Listening Only Matters If You Act

—— READ JAMES 1:12–27 ——

KEY VERSES

> *For if any are hearers of the word and*
> *not doers, they are like those who look*
> *at themselves in a mirror; for they*
> *look at themselves and, on going away,*
> *immediately forget what they were like.*
> *But those who look into the perfect law,*
> *the law of liberty, and persevere, being*
> *not hearers who forget but doers who*
> *act—they will be blessed in their doing.*
> JAMES 1:23–25 NRSV

UNDERSTAND

- What kind of situation do you think James was addressing in this passage of scripture?
- Why does James compare only listening to the Word of scripture to forgetting what you look like in a mirror?
- What kind of looking does James describe in this passage?

APPLY

A mirror offers a reality check. Whatever you may think about your appearance, a mirror always tells the truth. However, you can use a mirror to your benefit. A mirror may help you spot a problem so that you will be able to act. Looking into the mirror of scripture also works that way.

What James described is no passing glance at scripture. This is a very intent and deep look at the message of scripture that leads to liberty and freedom. What you see in scripture can change your life and lead to significant blessings and benefits. It may not be easy to obey scripture, but if you look at it closely and trust in the words that God has passed on to you, you'll be prepared to live an obedient life.

How you live your life today matters a great deal to God. He doesn't want you to be deceived about yourself. So look to the Bible for the truth about how to live. Plenty of other mirrors are available, but none is as clear and reliable.

PRAY

Help me, Lord, to trust in Your Word and in Your message for guidance in my life. May I take Your message to heart and translate it into obedient action that conveys my love for You and for others so that You gain the glory. Amen.

Never Too Late to Repent

───── READ 2 KINGS 23:19–25 ─────

KEY VERSES

*Furthermore, Josiah got rid of the mediums
and spiritists, the household gods, the idols
and all the other detestable things seen in
Judah and Jerusalem. This he did to fulfill the
requirements of the law written in the book
that Hilkiah the priest had discovered in the
temple of the Lord. Neither before nor after
Josiah was there a king like him who turned
to the Lord as he did—with all his heart and
with all his soul and with all his strength,
in accordance with all the Law of Moses.*
2 KINGS 23:24–25 NIV

UNDERSTAND

- In today's scripture reading, what is most notable about the way that Josiah responded?
- How do you think the people in Judah and Jerusalem responded when Josiah began to make the changes he knew needed to be made?
- What were some of the risks Josiah took when he made reforms based on the discovery of the books of the Law discovered in the temple?

APPLY

It's not easy to make a major change of direction in life. There are stubborn old habits to dislodge, and there may be fear of losses or mistakes. Family, friends, or colleagues may resist the changes you want to make. Yes, change can be hard—but Josiah shows that it is worth the effort to be single-minded and wholehearted in your pursuit of God.

Josiah could have given up in despair or shame when he discovered how far the people had strayed from God's commands. He surely wasn't popular with some people when he started removing household gods and longstanding customs. But God honors those who turn toward obedience with their whole heart, mind, soul, and strength.

You have an invitation today to turn to God in the same way Josiah did. Consider the areas of your life where you may have strayed away from God's commands or even the places where you've been unaware of what He expected. You can turn to Him today and make changes, even drastic ones, that set you on the right course. But, like Josiah, the best way forward is to make a clean break from disobedience and to follow God with all your heart, mind, soul, and strength.

PRAY

Lord, reveal the areas of my life where I have strayed from You, and help me to see a path forward through repentance and obedience. May I live in complete obedience to You throughout my day today. Amen.

Trust in God's Future,
Not in Your Past

—— READ ZECHARIAH 8:1-13 ——

KEY VERSES

"This is what the LORD of Heaven's Armies says: All this may seem impossible to you now, a small remnant of God's people. But is it impossible for me? says the LORD of Heaven's Armies. This is what the LORD of Heaven's Armies says: You can be sure that I will rescue my people from the east and from the west. I will bring them home again to live safely in Jerusalem. They will be my people, and I will be faithful and just toward them as their God."

ZECHARIAH 8:6-8 NLT

UNDERSTAND

- Why would God's people doubt that He could restore Jerusalem to safety as they struggled to rebuild the temple?
- How did past experiences shape the way the people of Jerusalem understood Zechariah's message from the Lord?
- How could the obedience and courage of God's people bring benefits to others as well?

APPLY

When you're rebuilding or starting over after a season of loss or suffering, it's hard to look forward in hope, even when God has promised good things. The sting of the past and the consequences of poor decisions can be overwhelming.

But how can you begin to trust God's hope for the future when everything in the present seems to be wrong? There aren't easy answers in today's passage. Zechariah asked the people of Israel to trust in God's message and to keep building things one day at a time. Hope doesn't come with the snap of a finger. You'll have to take a leap into the unknown and commit to the long-term work of faithfulness.

Yet as one day leads to another, God can bring change and renewal into your life. A new story can be written, and you'll find that the failures of the past are further in the distance as new memories take their place. As you find your way forward with God, your trust will be rewarded, and His faithfulness will become clear. What had seemed impossible can gradually lead to hopeful change and restoration.

PRAY

*Help me, Lord, to look at Your character and
Your promises with faith and hope so that
I can put my complete trust in You today.
May I find Your strength to live in obedience
and to write a new story of restoration that
rights the wrongs of the past. Amen.*

Courage Imagines a New Future

—— READ HAGGAI 2:1–9 ——

KEY VERSES

*"'But now take courage, Zerubbabel,' declares
the LORD, 'take courage also, Joshua son of
Jehozadak, the high priest, and all you people
of the land take courage,' declares the LORD,
'and work; for I am with you,' declares the
LORD of armies. 'As for the promise which I
made you when you came out of Egypt, My
Spirit remains in your midst; do not fear!'"*

HAGGAI 2:4–5 NASB

UNDERSTAND

- How does God speak to the leaders of Israel
  at a moment when the people are complaining
  about the failures of the present and the lack of
  hope for the future?
- Why is remembering God's past actions so
  important when seeking His guidance in a situation that seems hopeless?
- What hasn't changed for the people of Israel
  despite all of their failures?

APPLY

You may find yourself focused on the ways you don't
measure up today or the ways you've failed in the
past. But God is calling you to take a courageous
view of the future. Then you can find courage as
you look to the ways God has helped others and

on the promises He has made to you. Courage may not come easy or even feel natural.

Consider all of the ways that the people of Israel failed to listen to God and suffered exile as a result. Yet God's Spirit remained with His people. There was hope simply because God's faithfulness was far greater than the faith of His people. Just as the people couldn't go beyond the hope of God's restoration, you also can't move beyond a certain place without hope in the Lord.

It's easy to get weighed down by what others think. But God is calling you to make the courageous choice that asks, "What is God asking me to believe?" Despite what others say, there is a long history of God's people looking forward in hope, despite what seems like impossible odds.

PRAY

Lord, help me to ignore my doubts and the negative thoughts of others so that I can seek You and Your will alone. May I have faith in You to make the courageous choice that rests fully in You and Your faithful Spirit. Amen.

Praise God for Restoration

―――― READ PSALM 68:1-10 ――――

KEY VERSES

Father of orphans and protector of widows
is God in his holy habitation. God gives
the desolate a home to live in; he leads
out the prisoners to prosperity, but the
rebellious live in a parched land.
PSALM 68:5-6 NRSV

UNDERSTAND

- How does God treat those who are suffering and desolate?
- What in particular does this psalm of praise say about God's mercy and power?
- How could praising God change the way His people view others?

APPLY

Today's scripture reading asks readers to shift the way they look at others and what they expect from God. While God will punish those who rebel, there also is blessing for those who are suffering. Perhaps it's easy to overlook those who are suffering—or even to view them as afflicted—but God's desire is for the restoration of those who are most vulnerable.

The place where you can begin today is praise for God for His mercy and restoration. Just as God provided for the people of Israel in the wilderness and restored their lives, He desires to help those who are weighed down and burdened. You don't have to be worthy in any way in order to approach God with confidence and hope. God always shows His mercy to those in greatest need.

Look around today at those who are most in need or suffering. These are the people God wants to help and to restore. As you praise God for His mercy and justice, you can also shift your own view of suffering and seek ways to draw near to those who are at the heart of God's desires.

PRAY

*Lord, You are compassionate and kind.
Help me to see others the way You see
them and to approach You in prayer
with confidence and hope. Amen.*

Waiting for God's New Mercy

—— READ LAMENTATIONS 3:19–38 ——

KEY VERSES

> *I recall this to my mind, therefore I wait. The LORD's acts of mercy indeed do not end, for His compassions do not fail. They are new every morning; great is Your faithfulness. "The LORD is my portion," says my soul, "therefore I wait for Him."*
> LAMENTATIONS 3:21–24 NASB

UNDERSTAND

- What makes it possible to wait for God's mercy in the midst of suffering?
- How does making God your portion change the way you view the challenges of life?
- What makes waiting especially difficult?

APPLY

What comes to your mind as you endure suffering or difficulty? You may be so immersed in the lows of today that you struggle to imagine how things could ever get better. But they can!

The world and everything in it are passing away, but you can count on the renewal of God's love and mercy every morning. Waiting will pay off when you rely on a faithful God who will not and cannot forget His own people. When God is your "portion," you will always have something to look forward to even if you have to wait for what He has prepared for you.

When you walk through times of sorrow and loss, turn your eyes to God and His love, and consider how you can make Him your portion—the most important priority in your life. When you turn your gaze toward God, you'll find that His gaze has never left you. In that revelation, there is peace and patience abounding that can carry you through the darkest moments, moments that would otherwise feel lonely and hopeless. In God you have is a reason to look forward to each day with hope.

PRAY

Help me, Lord, to see if I'm relying on anything other than You. May I find peace and rest in the promise of Your mercy and compassion so that I can live with joy and peace as I endure even the most trying moments of my life. Amen.

God Answers Persistent Prayer for Justice

——— READ LUKE 18:1–8 ———

KEY VERSES

And the Lord said, "Listen to what the unjust judge says. And will not God bring about justice for his chosen ones, who cry out to him day and night? Will he keep putting them off? I tell you, he will see that they get justice, and quickly. However, when the Son of Man comes, will he find faith on the earth?"

LUKE 18:6–8 NIV

UNDERSTAND

+ Why would Jesus compare God's answer to prayers to an unjust judge who ignores a woman's pleas for justice?
+ According to Jesus in today's reading, what is the main problem for God's people?
+ What kind of approach should you take to prayer requests?

APPLY

Jesus wants His followers to long for justice, but He also challenges us to live by faith even when life is uncertain. Just as the woman in this parable didn't know if she was going to get justice, you don't know how exactly God will respond to your prayer. Yet Jesus wants you to rest assured that God hears your prayers and is far more compassionate than the unjust judge. The two things you don't know about God's response will be the *timing* and the *details*.

When Jesus tells His followers to be persistent in prayer, He wants them to realize that the problem in prayer isn't God's attentiveness but His people giving up too easily and failing to stay focused and intent on their prayer requests.

Although it's tempting to apply this passage to all kinds of prayers, Jesus specifically mentions the cause of justice and making things right. Whether that's a matter of injustice directed at you or the injustice someone else is enduring, this promise of God's attention to persistent prayer is specifically linked with setting things right.

PRAY

Thank You, Father, for Your attention to the cause of justice in the world and for Your compassion on those who are suffering. May I persist in prayer and share in Your commitment to make things right today. Amen.

Understanding Leads to Fruitfulness

—— READ MATTHEW 13:16–23 ——

KEY VERSES

"The seed falling on rocky ground refers to someone who hears the word and at once receives it with joy. But since they have no root, they last only a short time. When trouble or persecution comes because of the word, they quickly fall away. The seed falling among the thorns refers to someone who hears the word, but the worries of this life and the deceitfulness of wealth choke the word, making it unfruitful."

MATTHEW 13:20–22 NIV

UNDERSTAND

- ◆ What does it mean for someone who hears God's Word to be fruitful?
- ◆ Why is it not enough just to receive God's Word with joy in the first place? What gets in the way of joy?
- ◆ How do worries and the deceit of wealth prevent disciples of Jesus from being fruitful with God's Word?

APPLY

The words of Jesus have tremendous potential to change your life and the lives of others, but that change isn't going to happen without intentionality on your part. Life is filled with conflict and distractions. You can go off course easily, losing sight of

God's wisdom and chasing after something that feels good today but fails you over the long term. Part of the problem for those distracted by the cares of this life is the amount of time given to reflection on Jesus' teachings.

Today you can consider what it looks like to truly understand what Jesus has to say to you. You can pause and dig deeper into your own life today, asking questions or taking an inventory of your soul. What worries you? What do you desire? What are you seeking? There are plenty of ways to uncover what has taken root in your life rather than the words of Jesus.

Once you have an idea of the distractions and challenges you face, you may then consider the ways you can help the words of Jesus take root in your life. How can you keep His message in front of you so that you won't wilt under adversity or toss His promises aside when wealth promises security or prestige?

The fruit of God's Word shows up gradually, but if you invest time today in understanding the message of Jesus, you'll find new growth springing forth in your life.

PRAY

Jesus, help me to hear and meditate deeply on Your words of life. May Your new life rise up in me and lead to fruitfulness that draws me closer to You and prepares me to share Your promises with others. Amen.

God's Truth Isn't Always Easy to Share

—— READ JEREMIAH 28:5–15 ——

KEY VERSES

And Hananiah said again to the crowd that had gathered, "This is what the LORD says: 'Just as this yoke has been broken, within two years I will break the yoke of oppression from all the nations now subject to King Nebuchadnezzar of Babylon.'" . . .Soon after this confrontation with Hananiah, the LORD gave this message to Jeremiah: "Go and tell Hananiah, 'This is what the LORD says: You have broken a wooden yoke, but you have replaced it with a yoke of iron.'"

JEREMIAH 28:11–13 NLT

UNDERSTAND

- Why was Hananiah trying to deceive God's people, sharing a message that he had completely made up?
- What do you think the people listening to the two prophets made of the conflicting messages about deliverance from the Babylonians?
- What do you think compelled Jeremiah to share the bad news about Hananiah's false message?

APPLY

Sometimes the message from God isn't what people want to hear. You may be surrounded by people who are promising that everything is fine and there's no need to make any changes—in fact, things are about to get better! But God sees through attempts to hide sin and disobedience. There's no substitute for an honest assessment of yourself before God and an examination of where you are on the same page with God and where you've gone astray.

Jeremiah offered a challenge to face the brutal, difficult truth. The people of Judah should have repented and accepted the consequences of their unfaithfulness. They couldn't afford to keep limping along in disobedience before God. Yet smooth talkers like Hananiah had an audience because, like today, people don't like being told that they need to make major changes.

If you are willing to follow the example of those few people who listened to Jeremiah's message, you will be on the fast track to restoration and a new future. There's no point in trying to hide what God already knows. And once you come clean before God, you will be prepared to receive His blessings without anything getting in the way.

PRAY

Lord, help me to see my life with clarity and honesty as I come to You in prayer today. May I turn away from the easy answers and the simple solutions. I ask for wisdom to discern when I am in keeping with Your direction in my life. Amen.

Seek to Serve God above All Else

—— READ 2 TIMOTHY 2:1–13 ——

KEY VERSES

*Share in suffering like a good soldier of
Christ Jesus. No one serving in the army gets
entangled in everyday affairs; the soldier's
aim is to please the enlisting officer. And
in the case of an athlete, no one is crowned
without competing according to the rules.*

2 TIMOTHY 2:3–5 NRSV

UNDERSTAND

- What are the requirements of a soldier, and how did Paul apply them to the Christian life?
- Who are you most tempted to please in your life?
- Why is it so important for Christians to endure suffering?

APPLY

The goals of a soldier or athlete are clear and simple. Soldiers obey their commanders, and athletes channel all their energy toward competing for first place. A half measure or divided priorities simply won't work in these situations. You're either "all in" as a soldier or an athlete or ineffectively divided in your commitments.

Paul gave Timothy reminders about his simple Gospel message: "Jesus Christ, raised from the dead, a descendant of David." Jesus is alive, the fulfillment of God's promise to raise up a descendant of David to rule with justice and peace. No other person on earth is worthy of our allegiance, and no one else is as intimately aware of us.

Moments of suffering can truly test your commitments and even send you off track with your goals. Suffering may prompt you to look for the easy way out or tempt you to give up. There may not appear to be any point in enduring any longer. Yet if your goal is to win the prize of intimacy with God, then there's no question about enduring hardships. You may have to push yourself beyond what you think your limits may be, but if you can persevere to the end, no one can take God's reward from you.

PRAY

Jesus, help me to compete for the crown of life
You offer and to leave all other distractions
and misplaced priorities behind. May I become
entangled in only Your loving presence and the
work that You have set before me today. Amen.

Is Your Heart Fully Committed to God?

—— READ 2 CHRONICLES 16:7–14 ——

KEY VERSES

"For the eyes of the LORD range throughout the earth to strengthen those whose hearts are fully committed to him. You have done a foolish thing, and from now on you will be at war." Asa was angry with the seer because of this; he was so enraged that he put him in prison. At the same time Asa brutally oppressed some of the people.
2 CHRONICLES 16:9–10 NIV

UNDERSTAND

- What were the consequences of King Asa relying on his own plans to solve his problems?
- How could Asa have responded more constructively to the prophet's message?
- What does this passage teach about what God is looking for?

APPLY

If you'd like to become better able to confront the challenges you face today, the best course you can take is to address the state of your heart. What is your heart fully committed to right now? Answering that question can help you make an honest assessment of your spiritual state and whether God will be present to strengthen you.

If you persist in going your own way and relying on your own strength and plans, you can expect to be disappointed, even devastated. At some point you will either need to double down on your own ways and the consequences they bring, or you will confess your failures. Confessing the ways you've gone astray may be painful, but the sooner you turn back to the Lord, the sooner you'll be back on track with Him.

Even better, the Lord is looking for you to turn back to Him. You don't have to work to get God's attention or act in a certain way. Once you've shifted the orientation of your heart, you'll be ready for His loving gaze, which is already turned your way.

PRAY

*Lord, save me from the folly of my own
wisdom and the pitfalls of self-reliance.
May my heart remain fully loyal to You,
committed to Your guidance in my life. Amen.*

Faith Overcomes Fear

—— READ NEHEMIAH 4:11–20 ——

KEY VERSES

When I saw their fear, I stood and said to the nobles, the officials, and the rest of the people: "Do not be afraid of them; remember the Lord who is great and awesome, and fight for your brothers, your sons, your daughters, your wives, and your houses." Now when our enemies heard that it was known to us, and that God had frustrated their plan, then all of us returned to the wall, each one to his work.

NEHEMIAH 4:14–15 NASB

UNDERSTAND

- ◆ How did Nehemiah respond to the fear of the people when they worried about their enemies attacking them?
- ◆ Why did Nehemiah give God the credit for frustrating the plans of their enemies?
- ◆ What is the place of fear when trying to live by faith in God?

APPLY

In times of uncertainty, even threats to your well-being, the words of Nehemiah cut through the challenges of today: "Remember the Lord who is great and awesome." It's possible to lose perspective and forget who or what is great, awesome, or powerful. You may even feel like your afflictions are greater than God's power and presence.

Feelings of fear aren't unusual even for the man of God, but how we respond to fear and uncertainty will make all the difference.

Consider how Nehemiah reminded the people of God's power, emphasized their reliance on one another, and helped them get back to the work at hand—even if they had to carry weapons while on the job. The people kept working on what God had called them to do, but first they addressed the spiritual and physical elements of their situation.

Afflictions and opposition will come, but that doesn't mean the Lord has abandoned you. Such difficulties open opportunities for you to rely more completely on God's power and to examine the role of faith in your life. Through living by faith and trusting in God, you'll overcome fear by knowing that the Lord is with you.

PRAY

Help me, Lord, to see Your power and love with greater clarity than anything else in my life. May I commit myself to the work You've given to me and never fall away when adversity comes or affliction threatens my perseverance. Amen.

Seeking the Right Thing

—— READ MATTHEW 6:24–34 ——

KEY VERSES

*"No one can serve two masters. For you will
hate one and love the other; you will be devoted
to one and despise the other. You cannot serve
God and be enslaved to money. That is why
I tell you not to worry about everyday life—
whether you have enough food and drink, or
enough clothes to wear. Isn't life more than
food, and your body more than clothing?"*
MATTHEW 6:24–25 NLT

UNDERSTAND

* How does worrying about your needs impact how you approach the pursuit of wealth versus the pursuit of God?
* What line does Jesus draw between the pursuit of wealth as a master and the practical, everyday need to earn money?
* How could this passage impact the way you pray about your daily needs?

APPLY

Jesus went straight to the root of money's powerful entanglement, and His approach can offer you freedom. . .if you're willing to ask some difficult questions. His probing question "Why do you have so little faith?" addresses the need everyone feels for security and the struggle to trust God with it.

Money simply becomes a path toward security, making it possible to eat, to wear nice-looking clothes, and to live secure in a safe home.

The good news is that God knows what you need, and He has much compassion for you as you weigh the burdens of providing for yourself and others. He never leaves you alone, and Jesus assures you that relying on God's provision will pay off.

Relying on money for security can truly backfire, as it can become a cruel master. You will always wonder if you have enough, and your faith in money will replace your faith in God. You can have money while placing your faith in God, but you should always rely on Him, not money, as your source of security.

PRAY

Jesus, help me to bring my worries to You, trusting You to provide for me and leaving behind anything that isn't necessary. May I use money well for my own care and the care of others without letting it dominate my thoughts and desires. Amen.

Abundant Life Is Simple

———— READ JOHN 15:1–11 ————

KEY VERSES

"Remain in Me, and I in you. Just as the branch cannot bear fruit of itself but must remain in the vine, so neither can you unless you remain in Me. I am the vine, you are the branches; the one who remains in Me, and I in him bears much fruit, for apart from Me you can do nothing."
JOHN 15:4–5 NASB

UNDERSTAND

+ What kinds of spiritual practices can you do to "remain" in Jesus?
+ How does Jesus being the Vine and you the branch affect the way you view your own role in producing spiritual growth?
+ What does it mean to be "apart" from Jesus, and how can you prevent that from happening?

APPLY

Every follower of Jesus bears a measure of responsibility for his choices and actions, but Jesus makes it abundantly clear that you are not solely responsible for producing spiritual growth. Any changes in your life or growth in your spiritual awareness of God comes directly from Jesus. Any benefits that others enjoy because of your abundant life in God can be traced to Jesus' intervention in your life, not your own efforts or willpower.

Jesus invites you to walk a fine line where you must choose to remain in Him. There is a decision and an action in this. If you don't remain in Him, you will surely wither. But if you choose to remain in Him and put in the effort to keep Him at the forefront of your life, He will produce the life of God in you.

Jesus keeps it simple, telling His followers to cultivate a life of faith and dependance on Him. Once you are united with Him, your desires will begin to line up with His, and prayer will become much simpler because you won't have to worry about what to seek from God. The starting point is determining how you can ensure that you are abiding in Jesus today and every day.

PRAY

Jesus, You are my source of life and my hope for the abundant spiritual life You've promised. Help me to abide in You, remaining aware of Your presence and love so that I can bear the fruit of Your Spirit. Amen.

Hope in God Alone

—— READ PSALM 71:1–12 ——

KEY VERSES

In you, O LORD, I take refuge; let me never be
put to shame. In your righteousness deliver
me and rescue me; incline your ear to me and
save me. Be to me a rock of refuge, a strong
fortress, to save me, for you are my rock and
my fortress. Rescue me, O my God, from the
hand of the wicked, from the grasp of the
unjust and cruel. For you, O Lord, are my
hope, my trust, O LORD, from my youth.
PSALM 71:1–5 NRSV

UNDERSTAND

♦ What are some of the images used in Psalm 71
to describe God? What do those images mean
to you?

♦ What kind of adversity are you facing in your
life that could apply to the challenges described
in this psalm?

♦ What does it mean to be "rescued" by God in
your own circumstances today?

APPLY

The Psalms often use images of conflict and battle
to describe the threats and challenges of life that
oppose the security found in God. But you don't
necessarily have to be facing a personal enemy
or a difficult relationship to feel like you're in the

midst of conflict and in need of God's security. The enemy could be a medical diagnosis or a traumatic experience that haunts your thoughts. In each case, you may face adversity that makes it more necessary than ever to rely on God.

There are plenty of places where you can seek refuge. In fact, your greatest temptation may be relying on something other than God for protection in the midst of conflict, suffering, or uncertainty. That is where idolatry comes in, as you find yourself relying more on money, powerful relationships, or your possessions for security. An idol is anything that replaces the role of God in your life and keeps you from intimacy with Him.

Seeing God as your security and hope for the future is a process. Today's psalm tells us about learning to trust in God from the days of one's youth. It's never too soon or too late to start trusting God with the challenges of your life. It is something you learn and cultivate over time. But soon it will become natural to turn to God first when your life is out of sorts and uncertain.

PRAY

Father, You are the true refuge in times of trouble and fear. I can trust that I am safe in Your care because of Your mercy and Your enduring love for me. May I turn away from every false sense of security and rely on You alone. Amen.

The Lord Desires Peace for His People

—— READ HOSEA 2:14–23 ——

KEY VERSES

"I will betroth you to Me forever; yes, I will betroth you to Me in righteousness and in justice, in favor and in compassion, and I will betroth you to Me in faithfulness. Then you will know the Lord."
HOSEA 2:19–20 NASB

UNDERSTAND

- How did the Lord speak to the people of Israel in this passage even though they had been rebellious and unfaithful to Him?
- What does the image of being "married" to God imply about the kind of relationship God desires to have with you?
- How does God's compassion toward His people impact your view of Him?

APPLY

The sting of betrayal and unfaithfulness is difficult to endure, and the damage done is exceedingly difficult to repair. The key toward reconciliation for a broken relationship is for the betrayed party to extend forgiveness and compassion to the offending person.

In today's scripture reading, we can see God's compassion and mercy on display as He offered complete restoration and a new future of peace to the people of Israel even after generations of unfaithfulness and rebellion. God was eager to get a new start with His people, and the failures and sins of the past weren't going to get in the way of His plans for peace and unity.

You may feel the weight of your past failures and mistakes. Many people do simply because shame and guilt have a way of hanging around. While God wants you to take ownership of those failures, you can trust Him to restore you if you come to Him in confession and accept His forgiveness and mercy.

PRAY

Father, thank You for forgiving and restoring me so that I can move forward in faith and hope for the future. May I enjoy the peace You give Your faithful people. Amen.

Mercy Leads to Repentance

———— READ ACTS 3:17–26 ————

KEY VERSES

> *"Now, fellow Israelites, I know that you*
> *acted in ignorance, as did your leaders.*
> *But this is how God fulfilled what he*
> *had foretold through all the prophets,*
> *saying that his Messiah would suffer.*
> *Repent, then, and turn to God, so that*
> *your sins may be wiped out, that times of*
> *refreshing may come from the Lord."*
> ACTS 3:17–19 NIV

UNDERSTAND

* In what way did Peter give his listeners the benefit of a doubt in today's scripture reading?
* What does repentance and "turning to God" look like in your life?
* What is the promised result of Peter's listeners repenting from their sins?

APPLY

Humanly speaking, the apostle Peter had every reason to feel angry, even judgmental, toward the people who had either ignored Jesus' message or actively opposed Him. Yet he stuck with Jesus' mission to bring repentance and renewal, not condemnation.

It's not easy to talk to an indifferent or hostile listener about Jesus, but that is exactly what Peter did in Acts 3. After healing a lame beggar at the temple, he spoke to a group of amazed onlookers, many of whom had probably approved of the crucifixion of Jesus weeks before. Peter's example shows that mercy can win over judgment, as many of his listeners responded positively to his message.

God's mercy and kindness are well documented throughout scripture, and that kindness leads people to repent of their sins. Just as you have been forgiven by God, you can show the same mercy and forgiveness to others. In fact, Jesus expects just that.

It may feel good in the moment to condemn or judge others, but that won't lead to the refreshment that God desires for the world. The Lord has given each of us a holy calling to show others the path to God. The hope is that their sins can be wiped away for times of refreshing, but sharing that message can be challenging. The grace of God can feel risky and costly, but when others respond to it, it is well worth it.

PRAY

Jesus, help me to remember the ways You have shown grace and mercy to me, freeing me from judgment of others. May I show the same patience and mercy to others so that they can enjoy times of refreshing. Amen.

Use What God Has Given to You

—— READ MATTHEW 25:14–30 ——

KEY VERSES

*"Then he ordered, 'Take the money from
this servant, and give it to the one with the
ten bags of silver. To those who use well
what they are given, even more will be
given, and they will have an abundance.
But from those who do nothing, even what
little they have will be taken away.'"*
MATTHEW 25:28–29 NLT

UNDERSTAND

- The parable recorded in today's scripture reading talks about a master giving his servants money. What do you think God has given to you?
- How do you think you can "invest" the gifts God has given you?
- What is at stake in this parable concerning the gifts that God has given you?

APPLY

You may not believe that you have a lot to offer God or other people, but if you view your talents, abilities, and possessions as gifts from the Lord, then you have no reason to neglect them. Even the slightest ability or small portion of free time can be used well to serve or bless others. God has chosen to bless others through your abilities. In addition,

He will increase what you have so that you can reach more people for His purposes.

The servant in this parable who is called wicked and lazy didn't use the gifts God had given him and didn't have any plans to use them. The main issue here is neglect. If you neglect what God has given you, why should He give you anything else?

If you desire to be useful to God and a blessing to others, just ask Him to open your eyes to what He's given you, including the abilities you can use for Him. There are opportunities around you right now, and God wants you to use what He's given you to bless others and glorify Him.

PRAY

Jesus, help me to recognize the talents You have given to me. Give me the strength and determination to use them well for Your purposes and to glorify You. Amen.

God Responds to Changes of Heart

——— READ JONAH 3 ———

KEY VERSES

Then the king and his nobles sent this decree throughout the city: "No one, not even the animals from your herds and flocks, may eat or drink anything at all. People and animals alike must wear garments of mourning, and everyone must pray earnestly to God. They must turn from their evil ways and stop all their violence. Who can tell? Perhaps even yet God will change his mind and hold back his fierce anger from destroying us."
JONAH 3:7–9 NLT

UNDERSTAND

- In what ways did the people of Nineveh have more faith in God than Jonah?
- What kinds of changes did the king of Nineveh demand for his people?
- What could serve as a sign of repentance today?

APPLY

Jonah didn't hold out much hope for the people of Nineveh, and their change of heart after hearing the prophet preach shocked him. No matter how far you may have drifted from God, no matter how grievously you've sinned against God, and no matter how much shame you carry, you couldn't top the people of Nineveh. They were so wicked that God threatened to destroy their city.

But the Ninevites had a change of heart and repented—and God spared them.

God doesn't overlook a change of heart. If you come to God in repentance today, He will most certainly have mercy on you. There is no point too far from God. The Psalms speak of mourning being turned into dancing, and such a turnaround is always possible when God's people confess their sins and seek Him again.

When God saw the Ninevites' change of heart, He had mercy on them. But Jonah, who had reason to dislike the people of Nineveh, was angry because he hoped God would destroy them for their wickedness. Don't be like Jonah! Instead, when you learn that someone—even the worst sinner, the type of sinner who has ruined the lives of others—has a change of heart toward God, join all the angels in heaven in rejoicing over that saved soul!

PRAY

Lord, help me to remember that I am never far from mercy and restoration. May I always turn quickly to You after I have sinned so that I can receive Your mercy. May I show that same mercy to others who turn their hearts to You. Amen.

Endurance Comes from God's Power

—— READ COLOSSIANS 1:1–14 ——

KEY VERSES

*May you be made strong with all the strength
that comes from his glorious power, and
may you be prepared to endure everything
with patience, while joyfully giving thanks
to the Father, who has enabled you to share
in the inheritance of the saints in the light.*
COLOSSIANS 1:11–12 NRSV

UNDERSTAND

- What can you do to grow in your strength and endurance?
- How does giving thanks to God the Father in the midst of difficulties help you persevere?
- Why is it important to keep the rewards of obedience in mind?

APPLY

Endurance and patience for the trials of life aren't the kinds of things that come naturally. These are fruits of the Spirit that God can develop in you provided you actively seek them out and ask for them. The strength that God passes on to you has a divine source that you can't earn or develop through willpower. These are all gifts that are given to you based on God's grace.

Although these gifts come through grace, meaning God's unmerited favor, don't overlook the fact that Paul still prayed for these things to be manifested among the Colossian Christians. Being among God's people isn't a guarantee that you'll have instant access to all that God has made available to you. This is where intercession and requests are so important.

Jesus assured you that if you seek, you will find, and He promised that all who are thirsty will be satisfied. Paul's prayer is an invitation for you to actively seek more from God and to fully explore all you have been given through Jesus.

PRAY

> *Jesus, help me to endure the highs and lows of life with the strength and power You provide. May I keep in mind the hope of Your people who will one day share in Your inheritance because they relied on You above all else. Amen.*

Humble Faith in God

—— READ MATTHEW 8:1–13 ——

KEY VERSES

> *But the officer said, "Lord, I am not worthy*
> *to have you come into my home. Just say the*
> *word from where you are, and my servant will*
> *be healed. I know this because I am under the*
> *authority of my superior officers, and I have*
> *authority over my soldiers. I only need to say,*
> *'Go,' and they go, or 'Come,' and they come.*
> *And if I say to my slaves, 'Do this,' they do it."*
> MATTHEW 8:8–9 NLT

UNDERSTAND

- ♦ Why was it so important to Jesus that a Roman officer had so much faith in His power to heal?
- ♦ What made this Roman officer's request for a miracle stand out from others recorded in the four Gospels?
- ♦ How did this Roman officer correctly understand Jesus as a king with authority?

APPLY

Today's reading offers a helpful balance of faith and humility. Although the Roman officer knew that Jesus had the power to heal his servant, he also didn't think of himself as worthy to ask so great a thing of God's Son, even inviting Him into his home. In fact, his humility was only surpassed by his faith in the power of Jesus to heal.

It is a great and awesome thing to be able to ask things of God. Scripture offers the reminder that people are made from dust and will return to dust and also compares people to grass that quickly withers in the sun. You can make the mistake of assuming too much about your own importance and even end up making demands of God to meet your needs. When your prayers veer in this direction, the story of the Roman officer gives a helpful corrective.

By the same token, Jesus wants us to be bold and courageous when we make requests of God for ourselves or for someone else. No one standing alongside Jesus expected such great faith from a Roman officer, and so there's no reason why you too can't intercede in big ways for others. Prayers that put others first and proclaim that Jesus is King are the exact type that He longs to hear.

PRAY

Jesus, You are all-powerful and fully able to answer my prayers, bringing healing and restoration to those in need. May I never take Your kindness and generosity for granted as I pray for myself and for others. Amen.

God's Purpose Will Always Be Accomplished

———— READ ACTS 27:14–26 ————

KEY VERSES

"And yet now I urge you to keep up your courage, for there will be no loss of life among you, but only of the ship. For this very night an angel of the God to whom I belong, whom I also serve, came to me, saying, 'Do not be afraid, Paul; you must stand before Caesar; and behold, God has graciously granted you all those who are sailing with you.' Therefore, keep up your courage, men, for I believe God that it will turn out exactly as I have been told."

ACTS 27:22–25 NASB

UNDERSTAND

- What do you think it was like for Paul to trust that God's purpose for him was stronger than the power of the storm?
- Why did Paul speak so boldly to the crew of the ship?
- Where did Paul tell the crew on the ship to find their courage?

APPLY

When God has a mission lined up for you, there is nothing on earth that can stand in the way. Paul witnessed that in a most dramatic way while stuck in a life-threatening storm that eventually left him shipwrecked on a remote island. It's easy to get distracted by the circumstances all around you and the reactions of those in the midst of the storms of life as well. Others may be giving up all hope, and it will be tempting to follow their lead.

You can find confidence in what God has guided you to do and remaining faithful to it. If your life feels chaotic or lacking in direction, this is the day to quietly seek God's wisdom and guidance. Even if you feel like you're in a storm, God's mission for you cannot be overcome. You'll find peace and security in the assurance of God's calling.

When you enjoy the confidence of God's calling in your life, you can share that peace with others. They can learn to grow in their trust in God as you demonstrate faith and hope in uncertain times.

PRAY

> *Jesus, guide me in the choices I make today so that I won't fall into the trap of relying on my own wisdom. May I find Your path forward, and if I stray far from You, may I have the humility to correct my course. Amen.*

Look for God's New Thing

—————— READ ISAIAH 43:14–25 ——————

KEY VERSES

Thus says the Lord, who makes a way in the
sea, a path in the mighty waters, who brings out
chariot and horse, army and warrior; they lie
down, they cannot rise, they are extinguished,
quenched like a wick: Do not remember the
former things, or consider the things of old.
I am about to do a new thing; now it springs
forth, do you not perceive it? I will make a way
in the wilderness and rivers in the desert.
ISAIAH 43:16–19 NRSV

UNDERSTAND

+ Are you expecting God to do a new thing or to
  do only what you can imagine possible?
+ How could you begin to expect God to do something new?
+ How can today's passage help expand your
  understanding of God's power and strength?

APPLY

The Lord wants you to remember the things He
has done in the past, but we should also be on the
lookout for Him to do new things today as well.
God isn't content with you learning about the past
and stopping there. Each generation has its own
calling to be aware of Him and fresh challenges to
meet in the moment.

God's promise to do new things means that you have a calling to remain attentive and aware of what He is doing. Thankfully, it's not up to you to create the new things of God. You only need to remain aware of Him, pay attention, and follow where He leads you. Most importantly, don't be surprised if God's new thing feels uncomfortable or unfamiliar. If anything, that may be a sign that you're on the right track and needing to live by faith even more.

You can find hope in the story of God's people who also have had to leave the familiar behind and take up the path He had set before them. The Lord is great and powerful, and He will remain with you through the uncertainty of the days ahead.

PRAY

Lord, help me to rely on Your power and wisdom and not on my own understanding or ability. May I look beyond what I know and what feels comfortable so that I can move into the new thing that You've called me to. Amen.

A Countercultural Life

——— READ ROMANS 12:9–21 ———

KEY VERSES

> *Be devoted to one another in brotherly love;*
> *give preference to one another in honor,*
> *not lagging behind in diligence, fervent in*
> *spirit, serving the Lord; rejoicing in hope,*
> *persevering in tribulation, devoted to prayer,*
> *contributing to the needs of the saints, practicing*
> *hospitality. Bless those who persecute you;*
> *bless and do not curse. Rejoice with those*
> *who rejoice, and weep with those who weep.*
> ROMANS 12:10–15 NASB

UNDERSTAND

- ♦ How can you show preference to fellow Christians in brotherly love?
- ♦ Which of the actions in this passage do you find most challenging, and how can you experiment with incorporating them into your life a little bit more today?
- ♦ Why is it so important to bless those who persecute you and to overcome evil with good?

APPLY

Paul mapped out a series of practices for Christians that are extremely countercultural—and even counterintuitive. Giving generously to those in need and showing hospitality to others are two ways that have always been vital to supporting others. Both acts require faith that God will provide for your needs when you remain faithful and take care of others. It's surely more acceptable today to think of ways you can stockpile savings and other assets to protect yourself from uncertainty, but Paul said that Christians should be so devoted to the well-being of others that they give generously of their finances and homes to ensure that fellow Christians receive God's care.

Should hard times and even persecution come your way, the Lord doesn't want you to give up or to shrink back in fear. Cling to the hope He has given you, and continue to devote yourself to prayer. It's certainly not easy to endure hardships, but if you place your hope in God and continue to pray, you'll have the strength to continue.

The guiding principle for most of today's scripture reading is to seek the best for others, whether that's sharing in their joys or in their sorrows. Seek the best for others even when they curse you, blessing them in return. As you devote yourself to caring for others, you'll find freedom from the self-centeredness that ensnares so many today, and you'll draw near to God's heart for the world.

PRAY

Jesus, help me to see others the way You see them, care for their needs as if they were my own, and give generously to those in need. I trust that You can provide what I need in order to be generous and that You will care for me when I bless my opponents. Amen.

Godly Sorrow

—— READ 2 CORINTHIANS 7:2–12 ——

KEY VERSES

*Yet now I am happy, not because you were
made sorry, but because your sorrow led you
to repentance. For you became sorrowful
as God intended and so were not harmed
in any way by us. Godly sorrow brings
repentance that leads to salvation and leaves
no regret, but worldly sorrow brings death.*

2 CORINTHIANS 7:9–10 NIV

UNDERSTAND

+ What are the benefits that Paul attached to
  godly sorrow?
+ How do people typically view sorrow today?
+ How did Paul handle his responsibility to tell the
  Corinthians hard things while also encouraging
  them and caring for their souls?

APPLY

Consider how sorrow has impacted you. Perhaps
you still feel a lingering sense of regret or shame,
so you know that sorrow is hardly a pleasant experience. No one wants to mess up. And being the
person who has to point out the failure or misdeeds
of another brings a sense of sorrow.

Paul encouraged us to think of sorrow as a
catalyst for a fresh start. He held that we can
move on beyond our failures and the weight of our

sorrows if we're willing to go to the Lord and repent. In fact, Paul encouraged us not to dwell on our sorrows—beyond looking ahead to the ways we can make things right.

Moving beyond your sorrows today is a chance to open your life to God's healing and transformation. If you never want to feel the weight of sorrow again, you can imitate the determination of the Corinthians to change their ways. God is always ready to forgive and to aid those who are willing to turn to Him for a fresh start.

PRAY

Jesus, help me both to feel the weight of my sorrow over my sins and to move beyond my sorrow to the new life You offer as I repent. May I remember to show grace to those who are also moving through their sorrow and seeking Your renewal. Amen.

Mercy Belongs to Everyone

—— READ MATTHEW 18:21–35 ——

KEY VERSES

" 'Shouldn't you have had mercy on your
fellow servant just as I had on you?' In anger
his master handed him over to the jailers
to be tortured, until he should pay back all
he owed. This is how my heavenly Father
will treat each of you unless you forgive
your brother or sister from your heart."
MATTHEW 18:33–35 NIV

UNDERSTAND

+ Why does Jesus insist that His followers show mercy to others?
+ How does your treatment of others impact your relationship with God?
+ What does it mean to forgive someone "from your heart"?

APPLY

If you come to God in search of mercy and forgiveness, the good news of the Gospel is that the Lord is merciful and ready to restore your relationship with Him.

The debt described in the parable in today's scripture reading was impossible to pay back. Although the indebted servant was likely irresponsible and reckless with the money loaned to him, he still had the audacity to ask for forgiveness, and the master had the kindness to grant it. Even a massive debt is within the reach of God's mercy.

Grace and forgiveness should lead to transformation in how you relate to other imperfect humans. God expects you to dwell on the mercy and grace you have received. So, consider how lost you would be without His mercy, and then extend that same consideration to others who are in your debt.

Forgiving a debt can be costly. You may have to swallow your pride, and you may feel like someone has bested or exploited you in some way. Forgiveness doesn't mean that you need to be taken advantage of again, but you do need to let go of your right to demand some kind of payment for a wrong done to you. Holding on to unforgiveness is certainly a temptation, but it isn't an option when you have received God's mercy on such generous terms.

PRAY

Thank You, Lord, for the mercy You show in forgiving my debts and freeing me to serve You and others. May I show the same mercy and kindness to others so they can gain a glimpse of Your grace. Amen.

God's Justice Will Win

—— READ HABAKKUK 2:12–20 ——

KEY VERSES

> *"What sorrow awaits you who say to wooden idols, 'Wake up and save us!' To speechless stone images you say, 'Rise up and teach us!' Can an idol tell you what to do? They may be overlaid with gold and silver, but they are lifeless inside. But the Lord is in his holy Temple. Let all the earth be silent before him."*
> HABAKKUK 2:19–20 NLT

UNDERSTAND

- Why would people create idols and then rely on them for their security and prosperity?
- What are some examples of modern idols that people may rely on to save them?
- What are the differences between the people who rely on idols and the people who worship the Lord?

APPLY

The prophet Habakkuk warned his audience that the consequences for their reliance on false gods would soon be revisited upon them. That message also applies today.

There is no escaping the moment when God returns to earth to set things right. What you invest in today will be revealed for what it is on the day Jesus returns. There is no deceiving God, and so your best option today is to seek God with all your heart.

Consider that while some call out to their idols for help, the followers of the Lord are told to be silent before the temple. The Lord is present in the earth even if you can't see Him or look at an image of Him. You can only trust in faith that the Lord is with you and that you can't do anything to make Him more real or more present. The Lord will act to save His people and to bring justice to the earth, and nothing can stand in His way when the time comes.

As you pray today, consider where you place your trust and what you rely on. Then seek God's presence with quiet confidence. You don't have to shout for God to hear you. In fact, you may not need to say anything at all.

PRAY

Lord, You are the Creator of the earth,
the Keeper of the universe, and the
One truly just Judge who will one day
restore the earth. As I look to You in
silent adoration today, I am grateful to be
counted as one of Your children. Amen.

Effective Wisdom

—— READ ECCLESIASTES 9:7–18 ——

KEY VERSES

Now there lived in that city a man poor but wise, and he saved the city by his wisdom. But nobody remembered that poor man. So I said, "Wisdom is better than strength." But the poor man's wisdom is despised, and his words are no longer heeded. The quiet words of the wise are more to be heeded than the shouts of a ruler of fools. Wisdom is better than weapons of war, but one sinner destroys much good.
ECCLESIASTES 9:15–18 NIV

UNDERSTAND

+ Why is wisdom considered better than strength but many still neglect it?
+ How do the shouts of a ruler of fools, who is presumed to be a fool as well, drown out the quiet words of the wise?
+ What does it mean to you that one sinner can destroy much good?

APPLY

Wisdom is a powerful resource that comes from God's Spirit and can bring many benefits. While you likely aren't tasked with saving a city from an attacking army, the wisdom of God can have a tremendous impact in your life—if you value it and seek it out as if it were a precious treasure that could change everything for you.

Wisdom is a quiet power that is easily neglected and even scorned by those who pay heed to those who lead with loud shouts and agitating comments. Wisdom is often valued most when you need it desperately. But when other concerns take over in life, wisdom can fall by the wayside.

One of the most compelling reasons to cling to the wisdom of God is the potential damage sin can do. One sinner can destroy a lot of good, and so can one sin. Wisdom can help you spot the threats to your stability in the Lord. Without God's steady hand of wisdom guiding you forward, it's all the more likely that you'll go astray from His path for your life. But when you heed and live in His wisdom, He'll keep you on course.

PRAY

Lord, I ask for the guidance of Your Holy Spirit to lead me forward in Your wisdom so that I will not fall into the trap of sin or the ignorance of my own judgments. May I remember the benefits of Your wisdom and seek wisdom throughout my day today. Amen.

Where Are Your Roots?

—— READ COLOSSIANS 2:6–15 ——

KEY VERSES

> *As you therefore have received Christ Jesus the Lord, continue to live your lives in him, rooted and built up in him and established in the faith, just as you were taught, abounding in thanksgiving. See to it that no one takes you captive through philosophy and empty deceit, according to human tradition, according to the elemental spirits of the universe, and not according to Christ.*
> COLOSSIANS 2:6–8 NRSV

UNDERSTAND

- What are the advantages of staying rooted in Jesus?
- What is the role of thanksgiving in remaining rooted in Jesus?
- Paul was concerned about the influence of Greek philosophy on his original audience. What could be a comparable dead-end system of religious belief today?

APPLY

Having a strong start with Jesus is a great thing, but the apostle Paul wrote about the importance of making sure that you grow roots that go deep with Him. He wanted his readers to keep returning to the basics of the faith, such as loving God and living by faith. But he also wanted them to seek to go deeper by applying the teachings of Jesus to their lives and by learning to keep in touch with the Spirit.

It's easy for alternative belief systems to creep in and replace your roots in Christ. Whether that outside influence comes from a political system, philosophy, or a cultural movement, your roots in Christ must be tended and cared for, while the threats of other belief systems should be uprooted as soon as possible.

The idea of "living your life" in Christ may appear to be a vague concept. So how can you live "in" a God you can't see? It's most likely that Paul was referring to the orientation of your heart, desires, and mind. He wanted you to keep Jesus at the forefront of how you live each day, remaining mindful of Him and desiring quiet intimacy with Him.

PRAY

> *Jesus, thank You for receiving me and*
> *connecting me with the Father so that I*
> *can live by faith in Your care, love, and*
> *power. May I continue to rely on You and*
> *not any alternative foundation. Amen.*

Jesus Cares for Your Well-Being

———— READ JOHN 10:1–15 ————

KEY VERSES

> *"The man runs away because he is a*
> *hired hand and cares nothing for the*
> *sheep. I am the good shepherd; I know*
> *my sheep and my sheep know me."*
> JOHN 10:13–14 NIV

UNDERSTAND

- Today's scripture reading recounts a conversation between Jesus and the Pharisees. What point does Jesus make when He compares the good shepherd to the hired hand who runs away?
- What difference does it make in your life that Jesus is your Good Shepherd?
- What does it mean to you that Jesus the Good Shepherd knows you as His "sheep."

APPLY

As a follower of Jesus, you are His sheep and He is your loving shepherd. Being a part of Jesus' flock means that you follow Him and that He cares for you and protects you. In fact, Jesus is so committed to your well-being and safety that He is willing to lay down His life for you. Jesus doesn't lead you and protect you because of what He can gain for Himself—He leads and protects because He is genuinely committed to your safety and thriving.

There may have been moments in your life

when someone who should have cared for you didn't, preferring to place his own interests ahead of yours. But in the safety of Jesus' presence, you won't be neglected or discarded.

Jesus wants you to listen for His voice and to respond to it. There are many different ways to be attentive to Jesus' voice. You may be especially attuned to Him when you read scripture each day, or you may wait on the Lord in silent but hopeful expectation as you pray. However you listen for God's direction in your life, He will show up to lead you forward in very much the same way an earthly shepherd leads his sheep.

PRAY

Help me, Jesus, to listen intently and consistently for Your voice so that I can respond to Your call in my life. May I avoid the deception of self-serving hired hands and remain in the security of Your flock. Amen.

Love Leads to Generosity

―――― READ 1 JOHN 3 ――――

KEY VERSES

We know what real love is because Jesus gave up his life for us. So we also ought to give up our lives for our brothers and sisters. If someone has enough money to live well and sees a brother or sister in need but shows no compassion—how can God's love be in that person?

1 JOHN 3:16–17 NLT

UNDERSTAND

* How did John want his readers to apply the example of Jesus to their own lives?
* If John believed that generosity comes from the presence of God's love in our lives, how does someone receive God's love in the first place?
* What does today's scripture reading say about how Christians should treat one another?

APPLY

At the foundation of John's first epistle is God's love for you. If you are aware of that love and received that love, John wrote, then your life should be changed, different from what it was before. John offered the example of Jesus as both the *proof* of just how deep God's love is for you and the *example* of how to love others sacrificially. When you have the foundation of God's love built up within, you can then more fully express love and generosity to others.

John expected his readers to follow Jesus' example and lay down their own needs and desires for others, and he used the example of financial generosity to make that point. Christians should be aware of the needs of others, and when they are, the love of God will compel them to meet those needs. This type of concern for others is evidence that a person has truly been touched by God's love.

Your actions serve as the ultimate clue that you have received and been transformed by God's love. If you find yourself consumed with yourself, seek God and experience His love for you. Let the Lord transform you from the inside, and then the loving acts for others will follow.

PRAY

*Thank You, Father, for Your deep love for me
and for the sacrifice of Jesus on my behalf.
Thank You for seeking me when I was far from
You. May Your love transform my life and
enable me to more fully love others. Amen.*

Leave Judgment to God

—— READ 1 CORINTHIANS 4:1–13 ——

KEY VERSES

*I am not aware of anything against myself, but
I am not thereby acquitted. It is the Lord who
judges me. Therefore do not pronounce judgment
before the time, before the Lord comes, who will
bring to light the things now hidden in darkness
and will disclose the purposes of the heart. Then
each one will receive commendation from God.*

1 CORINTHIANS 4:4–5 NRSV

UNDERSTAND

+ Why would Paul write that he did not even judge himself but left the judgment to God alone?
+ What are the benefits of waiting for God to bring judgment on yourself or someone else?
+ How does God's knowledge of the hidden purposes of your heart change the choices you make today?

APPLY

Conflict with others can lead to assumptions, judgment, and second-guessing—and Paul was no stranger to that with the churches he founded. Although it's helpful to assess yourself, to evaluate your motives, and to listen to the advice of people you trust, Paul cautioned that these measures aren't the very best approach. In fact, escaping the scrutiny of others is hardly proof of innocence.

It is far more useful to examine your conscience before God and to seek to prove yourself before Him. There is nothing you can hide from God, and so you can believe that God's judgment will be true and just.

If thoughts of God's judgment leave you unsettled, just remember that you can trust in His willingness to forgive your sins and to wipe them away when you repent. When you "come clean" with God, you can be assured that you are free from judgment and don't have to live in uncertainty. Even better, when God's Spirit guides you, you will live in the freedom and peace Jesus promised His followers. That doesn't mean you'll be free from conflict and misunderstanding, but in the Spirit, you'll have the guidance God provides.

PRAY

Thank You, Father, for Your Spirit's guidance and for Your Son's sacrifice, which saves me from judgment. May I live today with purity of heart and intention so that I can serve others freely and bring unity to Your people. Amen.

The Best Fasting Benefits Others

—— READ ISAIAH 58 ——

KEY VERSES

"Is not this the kind of fasting I have chosen:
to loose the chains of injustice and untie
the cords of the yoke, to set the oppressed
free and break every yoke? Is it not to share
your food with the hungry and to provide
the poor wanderer with shelter—when you
see the naked, to clothe them, and not to
turn away from your own flesh and blood?"
ISAIAH 58:6–7 NIV

UNDERSTAND

* In today's scripture reading, what is the condition God gives for acknowledging His people's prayers?
* What does this passage say about the value of religious practice that tolerates oppression and ignores suffering?
* How could this passage change the way you worship God this week?

APPLY

There is certainly a place for "religious" practices such as fasting and humbling yourself before God in prayer, but in today's scripture reading, the prophet Isaiah tells God's people never to substitute these practices for dealing with injustice, oppression, and the needs of others. God is far more concerned with how you treat others than with the details of how you worship.

Putting this another way, caring for others is a kind of worship. If you want to demonstrate your commitment to God, care for others in the same way He cares for you. When you have abundance or extra resources, share them with others so that they can benefit from the blessings you've received.

The result of this kind of worship is that God will hear your prayers and honor them. If you are generous with others, God will be generous with you. In fact, you will find new dimensions of joy in God as you enter into the kind of life that God imagines for His people.

PRAY

Thank You, Lord, for Your generosity to Your people and for Your concern for others who don't yet know You. May I learn to care for others and to share from my abundance with them so they can benefit from the blessings You have so generously given to me. Amen.

The Rewards of Persistent, Humble Prayer

———— READ MATTHEW 15:21–31 ————

KEY VERSES

> She replied, "That's true, Lord, but even
> dogs are allowed to eat the scraps that
> fall beneath their masters' table." "Dear
> woman," Jesus said to her, "your faith
> is great. Your request is granted." And
> her daughter was instantly healed.
>
> MATTHEW 15:27–28 NLT

UNDERSTAND

- In what areas of your life do you feel the greatest need for Jesus to step in and help you?
- What does the story told in today's scripture reading teach about persistent, humble prayer?
- This story takes place during a time of tension between Jews and Gentiles. What should the Gentile woman's interaction with Jesus imply about welcoming people from other cultures as brothers and sisters in Christ?

APPLY

Humility and prayer go hand in hand. When you approach God, it is essential to know your place before your Creator. While God's mercy and grace are abundant, there also is no guarantee that your prayer request and God's desires are going to match up. So if you approach prayer with a humble understanding that God is not obligated to grant your request, it's actually more likely that He will grant it.

The story about Jesus at first ignoring a Gentile woman's desperate plea for help can feel jarring. But her persistence in the face of what seems like rejection teaches us that we sometimes have to stick with it in our prayers, knowing that God won't ignore us but may be waiting to give us what we've asked for. There's no magic number of days to persist in prayer. It's possible that we may have to persist in prayer for years before God moves on our behalf.

As you humbly seek God and bring your requests to Him, you can rest in His goodness and compassion. He welcomes your persistent prayers. One day, maybe not until you are in the glory of God's presence, you will see the rewards of your perseverance.

PRAY

Jesus, thank You for hearing my prayers and honoring my humble perseverance. Help me to continue to pray in faith for myself and for others so that we can draw closer to You and enjoy relief from our struggles in this world. Amen.

Blessings in Hardships

—— READ PHILIPPIANS 1:12–20 ——

KEY VERSES

What then? Only that in every way, whether in pretense or in truth, Christ is proclaimed, and in this I rejoice. But not only that, I also will rejoice, for I know that this will turn out for my deliverance through your prayers and the provision of the Spirit of Jesus Christ.
PHILIPPIANS 1:18–19 NASB

UNDERSTAND

- Why would Paul rejoice over his imprisonment and over those who were preaching the Gospel based on wrong motives?
- In what did Paul place his faith during his time of suffering and captivity?
- What was Paul's main goal in his ministry and how did that lead to freedom and joy?

APPLY

In Paul's letter to the Philippian church, he described a path to joy, freedom, and blessing that may seem counterintuitive. Yet Paul himself is an example of its effectiveness.

Paul endured suffering very few can even imagine. Yet he never complained but continued doing what God had called him to do—even in the face of sometimes frightening opposition. Through everything, Paul made the cause of the Gospel and the reputation of Jesus his top priority. Paul was our example of remaining focused on Jesus and His message no matter what it cost him.

This isn't to say that you should *desire* the kinds of struggles Paul endured. You can ask God to protect you from difficulties, but you should also be aware that He can meet you and bless you in the midst of hardship and struggles. God can work in you and for your benefit as well as the benefit of those around you in any life situation.

If you can link your desires with God's, you'll have a better perspective on life. When you care deeply about seeing other people enjoy liberty in Christ, the stakes of life will look very different. You'll find it easier to endure suffering and to find a silver lining in your struggles when you remember that God is with you through whatever you endure.

PRAY

Jesus, help me to leave behind my desire for an easy life so that I can better advance the cause of Your kingdom and share Your message boldly with others. Amen.

Sanctified to Serve

—— READ JOHN 17:1–19 ——

KEY VERSES

*"I am not asking you to take them out of
the world, but I ask you to protect them
from the evil one. They do not belong to the
world, just as I do not belong to the world.
Sanctify them in the truth; your word is
truth. As you have sent me into the world,
so I have sent them into the world."*

JOHN 17:15–18 NRSV

UNDERSTAND

+ What did Jesus mean when He said that His
  disciples "do not belong to the world, just as I
  do not belong to the world"?
+ How does being sanctified—made holy—affect
  the choices you make today?
+ Jesus has sent you into the world and prayed for
  your protection from the evil one. How does that
  encourage you and give you confidence today?

APPLY

If you belong to Jesus, you will always feel a bit out
of place in this world, which is filled with people
who hold different values than you and who aren't
guided by the Holy Spirit. If we're not careful, our
not belonging to this world can create adversarial
feelings toward those who aren't in a relationship
with Jesus. But that is counterproductive to the

mission Jesus has given you—namely, the command to go into the world to share His message of salvation through faith in Him.

God has made you holy by His Word and by the Holy Spirit so that you can reveal Jesus to others. For that reason, you don't conform to the standards of the world. Instead, you let Jesus transform your life so you can share that transformation with others.

Even though some will respond to you sharing the Gospel message with hostility, Jesus calls you to continue loving, serving, and sharing His message with others. You can find encouragement and empowerment to do those things because Jesus has prayed for your protection as you go about His mission in the world.

PRAY

Jesus, I ask for Your protection, transformation, and guidance as I go out into the world to share the hope of Your message with others. Help me to view others with compassion and mercy so that I can be an effective ambassador for You. Amen.

Chosen to Be Fruitful

—— READ JOHN 15:12–17 ——

KEY VERSES

*"You did not choose Me but I chose you,
and appointed you that you would go and
bear fruit, and that your fruit would remain,
so that whatever you ask of the Father
in My name He may give to you. This I
command you, that you love one another."*
JOHN 15:16–17 NASB

UNDERSTAND

♦ What did Jesus say is the purpose for your life
   as His follower?
♦ What condition did Jesus place on prayer
   requests to the Father?
♦ What did Jesus mean when He commanded
   the disciples to "love one another, just as I have
   loved you"?

APPLY

Jesus chose you to have a long-lasting impact in this
world. That means that you have the tremendous
privilege of praying to God as a beloved child as
well as the great responsibility to align your desires
and will to Jesus' desires and will. God has chosen
you to bear "fruit" for Him. That is part of your
identity as a follower of Jesus.

Jesus is so committed to helping you bear
fruit for Him and for the benefit of others that

He has given you the privilege of making bold prayer requests in His name. He promises that your heavenly Father will give you what you need to accomplish His purposes—if you simply ask in His name. Such a striking promise brings up the key issue at stake: Are your desires in line with Jesus and His will?

You have incredible access to God the Father because you have been united with Him through Jesus. What are you asking Him to do for you today so that you can bear fruit for Him?

PRAY

*Thank You, Father, for the incredible access
You have granted to me through Your Son,
Jesus. May my prayers remain in line with the
will of Jesus, and may I bear fruit that endures
for years to the benefit of many. Amen.*

Are Your Priorities Correct?

—— READ 1 CORINTHIANS 13 ——

KEY VERSES

*Now we see things imperfectly, like puzzling
reflections in a mirror, but then we will
see everything with perfect clarity. All that
I know now is partial and incomplete, but
then I will know everything completely, just
as God now knows me completely. Three
things will last forever—faith, hope, and
love—and the greatest of these is love.*
1 CORINTHIANS 13:12–13 NLT

UNDERSTAND

- What is the correct balance between the pursuit of spiritual gifts and the pursuit of love?
- What things did Paul tell the Corinthians to value above prophetic gifts and superior knowledge?
- How did Paul find comfort despite all the things he didn't know or understand?

APPLY

Paul knew that the Corinthians loved higher learning and spectacular spiritual gifts such as prophecy. While he certainly valued these things, he rightly worried that they had put their emphasis in the wrong place.

Consider today what you truly value. What is really important to you in your everyday life, especially your spiritual life? It's easy to get sidetracked by lesser priorities, to make side issues really serious sticking points that sow division in the church, which can cause different groups to take sides, choose leaders, and attack one another endlessly.

Paul's higher road involves faith, hope, and love, things he said would last forever. Faith means living each day in total dependence on God. Hope is a sense of unseen clarity about the future that places it in God's hands. Love, the greatest of the three, means both acceptance by a merciful God and a compassionate and accepting heart attitude toward fellow believers. We should never be so focused on gaining knowledge or spiritual gifts that we miss out on faith, hope, and love.

PRAY

Jesus, help me to put the lesser pursuits of spiritual gifts, prophecies, and knowledge in their proper places so that I can see the purity and power of Your love. May I receive Your love and then share it widely with others. Amen.

Gentle Instruction

—— READ 2 TIMOTHY 2:14–25 ——

KEY VERSES

*And the Lord's servant must not be quarrelsome
but must be kind to everyone, able to teach, not
resentful. Opponents must be gently instructed,
in the hope that God will grant them repentance
leading them to a knowledge of the truth.*
2 TIMOTHY 2:24–25 NIV

UNDERSTAND

♦ Think of someone who has departed from the
truth of Jesus. How do you view that person?

♦ Why would Paul tell Timothy to gently instruct
opponents? How could taking the risk of "going
easy" on someone in error pay off with a big
reward of repentance?

♦ How does Paul's belief that some opponents
are deceived by the devil change your view of
disagreements over beliefs and theology?

APPLY

Most people have a lot riding on their religious
beliefs. Many people's beliefs are shaped by their
personal experiences, stories, teachers, or relationships that nudged you in a particular direction. But
that doesn't make their views right. In fact, many
hold beliefs that are in absolute opposition to what
the Word of God says. These kinds of beliefs are,
in a word, *wrong.*

It's human nature to want to blast the views of an opponent to smithereens, to prove him wrong and yourself right. It may appear to be a win/lose situation where only the strong survive. Of course, you could "agree to disagree," but sometimes you'll meet people whose beliefs could do them genuine harm by leading them astray from God. Whether or not you believe they are under the influence of the evil one, you can do them a lot of good by putting your own ego aside and *gently* instructing them in God's truth.

When you talk with someone whose beliefs you know are not in keeping with God's Word, start by putting yourself in their shoes, be willing to engage that person by listening respectfully, and then humbly and gently answer his questions. Above all, remember that speaking the Gospel message isn't about you, it's about Jesus. You don't have to prove yourself right; you just need to speak God's truth.

PRAY

> *Jesus, help me to pursue the best for everyone I meet, especially those who oppose me or who may be in error. Help me to speak with gentleness and humility with others so that I can bring them closer to You and Your truth. Amen.*

Celebrate Generous
Grace for Others

—— READ MATTHEW 20:1–16 ——

KEY VERSES

> *"He answered one of them, 'Friend, I haven't
> been unfair! Didn't you agree to work all
> day for the usual wage? Take your money
> and go. I wanted to pay this last worker the
> same as you. Is it against the law for me to
> do what I want with my money? Should you
> be jealous because I am kind to others?'"*
>
> MATTHEW 20:13–15 NLT

UNDERSTAND

+ What is your reaction to the generosity of the
  vineyard owner in this parable?
+ Why does Jesus say the first will be last and the
  last will be first in God's kingdom?
+ How does God's generosity run counter to the
  expectations of society today?

APPLY

The workers in the vineyard who showed up late
needed to receive a full wage in order to feed their
families. While it technically would have been just
for the vineyard owner to pay them only for the
time they worked, such a small payment would not
have been very compassionate or in touch with
their actual needs. Yet the generosity they received

became a point of division with their fellow workers. Seeing mercy and grace shown to others may sometimes become a source of contention.

God sees how humanity has failed and is more than willing to treat people far better than they deserve. That may sound like really great news for you personally, but once you see someone else get the same kind of mercy, you may have a very different view of God. Is God merely giving others a free pass for their sins? Don't the commands of God matter?

Obedience does matter a great deal to God, but so do mercy and restoration. There isn't a limited supply of God's grace. In fact, everyone is treated with more grace than they deserve before God. Jesus doesn't want you to resent anyone else's need of mercy, because without God's grace, they'd have nowhere to go.

PRAY

Jesus, help me to remember the ways You have generously forgiven me and shown me mercy so that I am grateful to You and compassionate toward others. Amen.

Jesus Can Satisfy Your Desires

—— READ JOHN 6:25–40 ——

KEY VERSES

> *"For the bread of God is that which comes
> down from heaven and gives life to the
> world." They said to him, "Sir, give us
> this bread always." Jesus said to them, "I
> am the bread of life. Whoever comes to
> me will never be hungry, and whoever
> believes in me will never be thirsty."*
> JOHN 6:33–35 NRSV

UNDERSTAND

- How does Jesus' use of physical needs (food) help people understand their need for Him?
- What do you think the people talking with Jesus desired to receive from Him?
- What does it mean never to be hungry or thirsty when you come to Jesus in faith?

APPLY

Why are you following Jesus? It's a question many of His earliest followers had to confront. In today's scripture reading, many people wanted a steady supply of food so that they would never go hungry again. Although that's an understandable motivation at a time of Roman oppression, with droughts and famines sometimes making things worse, Jesus wanted them to know they were missing the bigger point of His ministry.

Jesus offers you a chance to consider what you crave today. You can examine your desires and consider whether they are drawing you closer to Him. It's possible that you crave something other than what Jesus offers. So do you truly believe that Jesus can give you something better?

The manna God provided in the desert sustained the people of Israel physically, but Jesus, the Bread of Life, offers to sustain you spiritually, leading you to a place of peace and restoration. Jesus is present with you, and much like a loaf of bread dropping from the sky into your lap, His Spirit has come to you so that He can be fully present with You.

PRAY

*Jesus, help me to move past the distractions
that draw me away from the fulfillment
and restoration You offer. May I find
satisfaction in You and in the spiritual
sustenance You offer. Amen.*

Whom Do You Trust?

—— READ JEREMIAH 17:5–12 ——

KEY VERSES

"But blessed is the one who trusts in the LORD,
whose confidence is in him. They will be like a
tree planted by the water that sends out its roots
by the stream. It does not fear when heat comes;
its leaves are always green. It has no worries in
a year of drought and never fails to bear fruit."
JEREMIAH 17:7–8 NIV

UNDERSTAND

- ♦ What would it look like to have spiritual security in the Lord regardless of your circumstances in life?
- ♦ What do you need to entrust to the Lord today?
- ♦ How does trusting fully in the Lord help you bear spiritual fruit?

APPLY

What you trust in will go a long way toward determining the amount of turbulence and turmoil in your life. You could trust in money or in powerful relationships, but both could disappear in an instant as they are very much at the mercy of life's circumstances. Ecclesiastes speaks of this approach to the world as a chasing after the wind. There is no foundation and no place to go for security when you trust in the unreliable resources of this world.

By contrast, trusting in the Lord leads to stability,

new life, and flourishing. Whether life is difficult or humming along according to plan, you can find a measure of peace and rest by relying on the Lord to direct your paths and to provide what you need. By growing in this trust, you can see your worries and fears fade away.

Besides the benefits you enjoy today by trusting in the Lord, you'll also be rewarded by God according to what you do. God is tuned in to what you're thinking and doing, and if you can live from a foundation of trust in the Lord, you can also look forward to the next life with hope and peace.

PRAY

Lord, I look to You as my source of stability, direction, and joy. Help me to remain rooted in You so that I am not tossed about by the shifting winds of life. May I rest in the confidence of Your reward, which is coming one day. Amen.

Beware of Overconfidence

——— READ LUKE 22:24–38 ———

KEY VERSES

*"But I have pleaded in prayer for you, Simon,
that your faith should not fail. So when you have
repented and turned to me again, strengthen your
brothers." Peter said, "Lord, I am ready to go
to prison with you, and even to die with you."*

LUKE 22:32–33 NLT

UNDERSTAND

- How do you think Jesus felt when the disciples claimed they would never abandon or betray Him?
- How should Peter have responded when Jesus predicted his denial?
- What do you think Peter expected would happen when he faced the possibility of death? What could have made him better prepared for that moment?

APPLY

Following Jesus can be a high-stakes calling that includes both human opposition and spiritual opposition. Like Peter, you may end up in a situation that is far more challenging and stressful than you ever could have predicted. And it's even possible that you will fail at the moment of truth.

One way to guard yourself from opposition is to avoid overconfidence, to humbly assess your weaknesses and confess your struggles to God. Don't assume you'll always make the right choice or always remain on the right path. Straying from the truth—or at least making a big, costly mistake—is a very real possibility.

While you should keep your own weaknesses in mind, the other side of the story is Jesus' intercession for Peter. He will stand by you as well, interceding on your behalf and coming alongside you to help you when you feel like you can't go on (see Hebrews 7:25). And if you should fail, He will restore you—just as He restored Peter at his lowest point of shame and grief.

PRAY

Jesus, help me to view my weaknesses with honesty and clarity so that I can remain careful and attentive while also trusting You to support me when I'm struggling. Amen.

Share What You Have Received from God

—— READ 1 PETER 4:1-11 ——

KEY VERSES

Above all, maintain constant love for one another, for love covers a multitude of sins. Be hospitable to one another without complaining. Like good stewards of the manifold grace of God, serve one another with whatever gift each of you has received.
1 PETER 4:8-10 NRSV

UNDERSTAND

- Why did Peter place love above all else?
- Why did Peter spell out the need to show hospitality to others without complaining?
- How did Peter say you should use the gifts God has given you?

APPLY

The grace of God is a gift you have been given, but Peter knew that there's a good deal of work and intention that goes into fully enjoying and sharing that gift from the Lord. Prayer requires discipline to keep it a top priority, and love calls for perseverance when those around you are engaged in sin. Hospitality will be inconvenient, but it has long been a way to honor others and to care for their needs.

By calling God's people "stewards" of God's grace, Peter was making a point that grace isn't just for us to keep for ourselves but a gift we should share readily. You have been blessed because God sees the potential in you to carry his influence to others. He sees the potential in you for love, generosity, and peace. When you care for others, you release to them the kindness that God has already given to you.

Your invitation from God today is to find new ways to bless others with the love and mercy He has given you. Along the way, you'll find that people are likely to share that same love and mercy back to you.

PRAY

Jesus, help me to see the love, grace, and favor You have bestowed on me. May I recognize Your gifts and freely share them with others, disciplining myself to pray and to love others with generosity. Amen.

About the Author

Ed Cyzewski is the author of *Reconnect: Spiritual Restoration from Digital Distraction* and *Flee, Be Silent, Pray: Ancient Prayers for Anxious Christians.* He is the coauthor of *Unfollowers: Unlikely Lessons on Faith from Those Who Doubted Jesus.* He writes about prayer and imperfectly following Jesus at www.edcyzewski.com.